The Key to Egypt
including the Red Sea

REG BUTLER

In Association with

THOMSON HOLIDAYS

SETTLE PRESS

While every reasonable care has been taken by the author and publisher in presenting the information in this book, no responsibility can be taken by them or by Thomson Holidays for any inaccuracies. Information and prices were correct at time of printing.

3rd edition 1997

First published by Settle Press
10 Boyne Terrace Mews
London W11 3LR

ISBN (Paperback) 1 872876 55 2

Printed by Villiers Publications
19 Sylvan Avenue
London N3 2LE

Maps and line drawings by Mary Butler

Foreword

As Britain's leading holiday company operating to Egypt, Thomson are happy to be associated with Reg Butler's book 'The Key to Egypt including the Red Sea'. In writing the book, the author worked closely with our resident representatives who have year-round contact with holidaymakers' travel interests.

Whether you have chosen a cruise or a one- or two-centre package, we feel this pocket book can act as a quick reference guide to Egypt's enormous sightseeing riches.

It's impossible to see everything in one or two weeks. When the holiday is over, we suggest you keep this guide-book to help plan your return visit.

All prices mentioned in the text were accurate at the time of printing, when the exchange rate was around 5.3 Egyptian pounds to the pound sterling, or 3.3 Egyptian to the US dollar. But Egypt has an inflation problem, and local prices will certainly change during the coming year. However, any costs quoted in the book can serve as guidance to the average level of expenses.

THOMSON HOLIDAYS

Contents

CITY & SITE PLANS

Chapter One
Introducing Egypt

1.1 Journey through 5,000 years

Tourism to Egypt started with a flourish over a hundred years ago, based on organised winter visits to the ancient Egyptian sites. Luxor and Aswan especially developed as leisured winter resorts due to their dry and warm climate. In Upper Egypt it rains about three days a year, for a few minutes.

Today, the emphasis has broadened away from winter warmth, with Egypt firmly established as a year-round destination that also caters for the suntan trade. Direct charters from Britain to Luxor have opened up a 'different' resort destination, using hotels with luxuriant gardens that reach to the river's edge.

Likewise, Nile cruising is now a year-round experience. Over 200 well-equipped cruise boats with full air conditioning ply mainly on the popular reaches between Luxor and Aswan. Some of these vessels are operated by hotel chains like Hilton, Sheraton and Marriott — setting high standards for virtually the entire river fleet. All the boats operate like sedate floating hotels, with smiling service, good food and comfortable cabins.

Shorter trips are based particularly at Luxor, offering every variation from two-day to seven-day itineraries. It's an idyllic form of travel, cruising peacefully along the river with sightseeing spells ashore. There is enormous contrast of life-style compared with that of Cairo — laid-back and relaxed, compared with the hectic life of the capital.

Temperatures go higher, the further south up the Nile Valley. At the awe-inspiring ancient sites of Luxor, mid-day winter temperatures reach the eighties; so most tourists start their sightseeing promptly after an early breakfast. There's no need for a brolly in Upper Egypt, unless to use as a parasol. Even though temperatures can top 100° F, air conditioning provides a cool retreat for siesta time.

Delightful white-sailed yachts, called feluccas, can be hired for a few hours, or a day. For the young at heart in the 20-35 age-band, feluccas can even be used for adventure cruises — bring your own sleeping bag! Duration of journey depends on strength of winds.

Cairo tourism revolves particularly around the Pyramids of Giza and on the superb Egyptian Archaeological Museum which is mind-blowing in its riches. In recent years, the Sphinx and the Great Pyramid have been rivalled by interest in the Solar Boat — a 141-ft royal vessel. Claimed as the world's oldest surviving boat, it gives an insight into the grandeur of the Pharaohs' life-style.

Cairo can be something of a culture shock: mosques around every corner, tiled fountains, entire bazaar sections devoted to various crafts and trades. Strings of camels lope in to market. But Cairo is also Africa's largest city of over 15 million people, with fast-flowing traffic that speeds along elevated highways, through tunnels and across the wide Nile bridges. High-rise hotels and office blocks are as modern as anything in the western world.

In Cairo you can experience 4,000 years of history — ancient Egyptian, Christian, Islamic, Ottoman and 20th-century. There's infinitely more to Cairo than Pyramids, Sphinx and the golden treasures of Tutankhamun!

Despite the ease of taking even a short break in Egypt, it's certainly not a mass tourist destination. In a land of such rich history, it's worth doing some background reading to get better understanding of what Egypt can offer.

There is great fascination in the story of the Nile itself. Its life-giving role has reached from the earliest human development of agriculture. Today the tamed river helps feed 50 million people, while producing electricity that powers modern industry.

Read how the forgotten code of the hieroglyphs was cracked, to open up history and myth like a book, onwards from 3,000 BC. Egyptologists can interpret for us every detail of the social life and beliefs of the pharaohs, priests, gods, bureaucrats, builders, craftsmen and farmers. Fascinating!

Although Egypt is well embarked into the 20th century, the travel experience is closer to the Orient than to the hyper-efficient West. A visitor is cocooned, observing the local life-style from behind air-conditioned windows. But sometimes the standards falter.

Flights can be delayed or even cancelled. Sometimes there are traffic jams on the Nile locks, and itineraries may have to be adjusted and mealtimes rearranged. But your journey through 5,000 years of history will be made in 20th-century comfort.

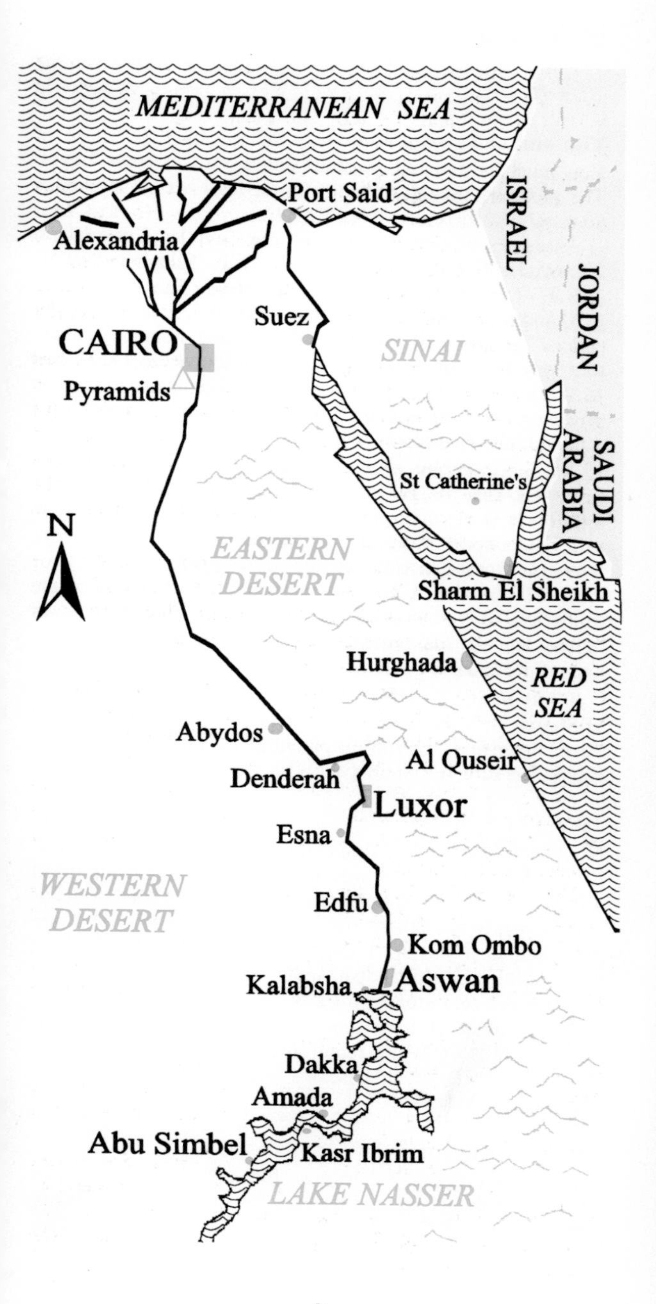
MEDITERRANEAN SEA
Port Said
Alexandria
ISRAEL
JORDAN
Suez
CAIRO
SINAI
Pyramids
SAUDI ARABIA
St Catherine's
N
EASTERN DESERT
Sharm El Sheikh
Hurghada
RED SEA
Abydos
Al Quseir
Denderah
Luxor
Esna
WESTERN DESERT
Edfu
Kom Ombo
Kalabsha
Aswan
Dakka
Amada
Abu Simbel
Kasr Ibrim
LAKE NASSER

1.2 At your service in Egypt

Visa and entry regulations

You must have a full passport and a visa to enter Egypt. The passport should be valid for at least six months after your scheduled return from Egypt.

Visas can be obtained through the Egyptian Consulate at 2 Lowndes Street, London SW1X 9ET. Telephone: 0171-235 9777 or 9719. Fax: 0171-235 5684. The visa cost is £15, and a passport-sized photo is required. Personal applications can be made between 10 a.m. and 12 noon; collection on the next working afternoon between 14.00 and 15.00 hrs. Postal applications can take much longer to process. The visa will be valid for the next 3 months for a maximum one-month visit.

If time does not permit obtaining a visa before departure, it's easy to get one on arrival at Cairo or Luxor airport. It works quite smoothly. Before you present yourself to Passport Control, you'll see a line of exchange bureaux which can sell you a visa stamp for US $ 15 or £10. That's also a convenient time for changing some funds into Egyptian currency. Be sure to check the notes before leaving the bureau, as sometimes the bank clerks happen to make a counting error.

Caution: if you are flying by direct charter into Sharm el Sheikh, a visa obtained on arrival is valid only for the Sinai Peninsula. If you're planning to visit elsewhere in Egypt, be sure to obtain your visa from London.

Jabs

No vaccination certificates are required. Some medical people lean heavily towards ultra-caution, and recommend a full range of inoculations against Typhoid, Polio, Tetanus and Hepatitis A. Others suggest that these precautions are not essential if you are taking normal care of yourself, and not visiting any outlandish areas. Most visitors to Egypt are exposed to virtually nil risk. However, ask your own doctor's advice at least four weeks before departure. For further details on health requirements for Egypt contact the Hospital for Tropical Diseases Healthline on 0839 337 722. Code number 22.

Arriving in Egypt

Leading tour operators arrange for a local travel agency rep to give escort service through passport control. Thomson clients should look for the Eastmar representative. Non-Egyptian travel staff are not allowed inside the airport building. UK reps will meet you outside the Terminal.

Customs, and currency regulations

Customs: It is no longer necessary to declare your foreign currency. But a video camera must be declared, and details entered into your passport.

Currency: You are not permitted to import more than LE 100 (see below) in Egyptian currency. Likewise, export of any quantity of Egyptian currency is forbidden. Before departure, be sure to finish up your soft Egyptian pounds, or re-exchange them on production of an original exchange receipt. Egyptian banknotes have little exchange value once you've left the country.

There's no longer any obligation to exchange a minimum sum into Egyptian pounds on arrival. But payment for accommodation in top-grade hotels must be backed by proof that the Egyptian pounds have been legally exchanged.

What is the currency?

The Egyptian pound (written as LE or £E, and pronounced *ginay*) is divided into 100 piastres. As a rough guide, reckon five Egyptian pounds to the pound sterling, or three to the dollar. But check the exact exchange when you travel, as the rates are constantly changing.

Coins are in denominations of 5 and 10 piastres, but you rarely meet them. Notes are in denominations of 25 and 50 piastres and LE 1 (coloured brown), 5 (blue), 10 (red), 20 (green), 50 (brown) and 100 (blue-green). There's always a shortage of small-value notes, and cabbies and street vendors often profess acute problems in making change. So try to keep a stock of small money, which also comes in useful for *baksheesh*.

Banks are open daily except Friday and Saturday. Opening hours vary but are approximately 9.30 am — 2.00 pm from Monday to Thursday and 9.30 am — 12.00 noon on Sunday. Exchange facilities in hotels are usually open every day. A plus point for Egypt is that exchange rates are the same everywhere, and you are not scalped by commission.

Under no circumstances should you change money on the black market. It is illegal and tourists are an easy target for cheats. If you are Nile cruising, exchange facilities are available only while the boats are moored in Luxor and Aswan.

We suggest that you take sterling or dollar travellers cheques plus some currency in cash. Keep the exchange receipts, which are needed to settle hotel extras in Egyptian currency, and to reconvert surplus Egyptian currency. Don't change more than you intend to spend. Most hotels and cruise boats now accept the usual major international credit cards such as MasterCard, American Express and Visa. Consult your representative on arrival. Most hotel cashiers now also accept Euro-cheques. But you may have problems in trying to withdraw cash on a credit card.

What to pack for sightseeing

A torch is very useful for visits to the tombs plus an insulated bottle or thermos for keeping drinks cool. A sun hat, sunglasses and high factor sunscreens are essential. Binoculars are certainly worth taking on a cruise.

What to wear

Informal, comfortable clothing with sensible walking shoes or trainers for sightseeing. In winter you will need light woollens plus a coat or anorak for evenings. Midwinter in Cairo can also be quite cold during daytime — affluent Cairo women wrap up in fur coats!

In summer light cottons are advisable, but bring a sweater for the evenings, when temperatures can drop quickly. After a day in the 90's, an evening temperature of 70 degrees can feel chilly!

When visiting mosques, it's unacceptable to wear shorts or sleeveless dresses. In general, out of respect for local customs, wear conservative dress when outside normal sunbathing areas. Women should not wear revealing clothes.

Casual dress is OK on cruises, and evenings are informal. A jacket and tie or cocktail dress are not essential.

Hotels and all cruise boats have a laundry and pressing service.

Phoning home

International calls can be made from a hotel or telephone office, although it may take some time to get through, despite direct dialling. The code for U.K. is 00 44 followed by the area code (STD) and then the number. The initial zero should always be omitted from the STD code. Thus, when calling London (0171), dial 00 44 171 and then the local number.

Calls from a hotel are very expensive and reverse charge calls are not possible. To avoid a horrible shock, first ask the hotel the cost of a 3-minute international call.

It is cheaper to ring after 8.00 pm. Some computerised hotel systems will charge even for an unanswered call if it rings more than 4/5 times. Be aware.

Calls from Britain to Egypt are also high-cost — more than double the price of phoning North America. From the UK to Egypt, dial 00-20, followed by 2 for Cairo; 95 for Luxor; 97 for Aswan; or 62 for Sharm El Sheikh.

Local transport

Air

Domestic air links are operated by EgyptAir, making it very easy to compile two-centre holidays. From Luxor, Aswan or Sharm El Sheikh it's feasible to make brief one-day or two-day trips to see Cairo and the Pyramids.

Rail

From Cairo, express trains operate to Alexandria, Luxor or Aswan at very modest cost. Air-conditioned sleepers offer luxury-grade transport between Upper and Lower Egypt.

Nile cruises

Even if you haven't made advance arrangements, it's often possible to arrange a sampler one-day or two-day excursion from Luxor. Ask your travel-agency rep.

Road travel

For security reasons, road transport including coaches often takes longer than expected, owing to the operation of a convoy system designed for the safety of visitors.

Feluccas

All three main locations — Cairo, Aswan and Luxor — are ideal for a classic hour or two aboard a felucca: the lateen-rigged sailing vessel which has plied the Nile for centuries.

Remember that you need a reasonable wind to get best value. If there's no wind, you'll find yourself switched to a motor launch, which doesn't have the same evocative atmosphere. Wait for better wind another day.

Obviously you have to bargain. Make it crystal clear that you're agreeing to a price in Egyptian pounds, and that it's for the entire boat, regardless of how many other passengers.

With price established, it's still very hard to resist the plausible arguments for baksheesh on top. Never pay up-front! At the end of the journey, there's no reason why you shouldn't just pay the agreed price and walk away, shutting your ears to the inevitable pitch for more money. But it's all done in the most friendly possible spirit.

Remember that you are the boss of the routing, and establish clearly how long the trip should last, and how long you want for any sightseeing stops ashore. Otherwise there will surely be supplementary demands for 'waiting time'.

Taxis and Carriages

In Luxor and Aswan, taxis and horse-carriages are very cheap by UK standards, and LE 5 should more than cover any brief trips. Even when you have firmly agreed with a carriage driver for a fixed price and no baksheesh, he may still smilingly suggest "baksheesh for the horse." Using taxis for longer-distance sightseeing demands fierce haggling, and a firm agreement on price.

Cairo transport

Cairo buses are extremely crowded and very grubby: not recommended except for hard-up backpackers. Infinitely better is the city's Metro system which opened in 1987. However, the traveller has choice of only two directions: northeast to the suburb of El Marg, or south to Helwan. Tickets are extremely low cost. The subway is spotless.

The Metro is best used for visiting Coptic Cairo. Just travel four stops from Sadat Station on Tahrir Square, to Mari Girgis. The entrance to the Coptic Museum is immediately opposite the station.

Otherwise, for short-haul journeys in central Cairo, taxis are best, and are easily hired in the street. Meters are more for decoration than use. Virtually a three-level payment system prevails. For an average ride in central Cairo, a local Egyptian would expect to pay LE 1; an expatriate who knows the ropes would pay LE 3; and a tourist engaging a taxi from a hotel cab-rank wouldn't get away with less than LE 5.

It's claimed that doormen at leading hotels require a pay-off from each cabby of LE 2 for the right to queue in the cab-rank. Hence the higher price, but possibly a cleaner and more reliable vehicle, with a driver who has some English.

If you hail a passing taxi, *don't* follow all the usual rules about haggling for an agreed fare in advance. At the end of the journey, have the exact money ready — such as LE 3 for a short to medium distance. Hand it over and walk off without further comment. The cabby will just assume you know the going price for an ex-pat, and usually there's no argument, and no need for extra baksheesh. Remember you are still paying more than the locals.

Electricity

The current in Egypt — both in hotels and aboard cruise ships — is 220 volts. Sockets are the European type with two round plugs. Pack a plug adaptor if you expect to use your own electric gadgets, such as shaver or hairdryer. Continental adapters are obtainable in most electrical and D.I.Y. stores, Woolworth's, or at your departure airport.

Time Change

Except for short periods in spring and autumn, when changeovers of Daylight Saving Time are not synchronised, Egypt is two hours ahead of UK time; seven hours ahead of US Eastern Standard Time.

Medical

If you're going to Cairo, Luxor or Aswan, the malaria risk is virtually nil. But protection tablets are recommended if you are visiting the Nile Delta between June and October. If you feel unwell during a 3-months' period after your visit, mention Egypt to your doctor so that he can make an appropriate test.

The more usual Egyptian problem is a two-day attack of Tutankhamun's Revenge, aka diarrhoea. The principal hotels, cruise-boats and restaurants offer safer eating and drinking, using water that has been filtered and boiled. A flask of reliable water is placed in every bedroom. City tap water is safe, but heavily flavoured with chlorine.

Outside the hotels, you'll enjoy better odds if you ensure that bottled water sold by street vendors has an unbroken seal (it's not unknown for bottles to be refilled from the tap), and avoid ice cream, salads, or fruit which you haven't peeled yourself. Ensure that food is freshly cooked, and not re-heated. Most upsets are caused by unaccustomed spicy food, cold beers and hot sun. Wash fruit carefully, and consume any iced drinks before the cubes have dissolved.

If the bug hits, doctors advise drinking plenty of fruit juice — such as lemon, orange or lime — or bottled water with a twitch of sugar and salt (to counter dehydration). Continue eating normally. Among the pharmaceuticals, Lomotil, Imodium and Arrêt are usually effective.

Local doctors can provide stronger preparations if necessary.

Salt tablets, boiled sweets and dehydration sachets are worth packing in your luggage. A small first aid kit could also include plasters, antiseptic cream, and anti-insect cream (before and after).

To ensure a peaceful sleep, night-flying insects can be outwitted by keeping bedroom windows closed and air conditioning switched on. It's worth packing an electrically-operated mosquito kit, which can be remarkably effective.

Finally, avoid petting stray dogs. Rabies is endemic.

If you need medical attention, please contact reception or your local rep who will call an English speaking doctor. Keep any receipts for medication or consultation if you plan to reclaim from insurance.

WC problems

You have to be desperate to use the facilities in the average town or wayside café. Sometimes the gap between utter misery and fulfilment is measured by a few sheets of toilet paper. Always carry a few spare sheets in your holdall, in case of emergencies.

Sun and health

Deep suntan is often regarded as a sign of health, but doctors advise caution against overdoing it, because of skin-cancer risk. Against sunburn, the standard advice is well enough known. But many holidaymakers don't fully realise the power of the Egyptian sun, which can still burn even if you're sitting in the shade, where bright sunshine can be reflected off water or sand. Ultraviolet rays can also strike through clouds, though a heavy overcast sky does offer some protection.

A standard rule is to avoid the UV danger time between noon and 2 p.m. Take extra care whenever your shadow is shorter than your height. The shorter your shadow, the more risk of sunburn.

Take the sun in very small doses for the first few days. Especially for sightseeing in hotter months, always wear a wide-brimmed floppy sun hat, or a baseball-type cap.

For sunbathing, use plenty of high-factor suntan lotion — SPF of 15 or over — reapplied every hour or so after you've been in the pool. Try doing your sunbathing late afternoon when the sun is not so strong. Wear a T-shirt while swimming or snorkelling. If your exposed skin has turned pink or red by evening, be more careful next day!

In case of heatstroke — marked by headache, flushed skin and high temperature — get medical advice. Meanwhile wrap yourself in wet towels, and drink fruit juice or water.

Finally, beware of iced drinks while sunbathing, and then jumping in the pool. Your tummy is bound to rebel.

News

The London newspapers arrive in the principal cities a day or two after publication. Typical newspaper prices are well over £1 sterling for the heavy dailies. *The Guardian*, printed in Frankfurt, is somewhat cheaper, around LE 4.

There is one local English-language daily newspaper — the *Egyptian Gazette*, costing 50 piastres. It carries wire-service world news — heavily slanted towards Arab viewpoints — some tourist items, and timings of the day's events such as Sound and Light shows.

Every Thursday *Al-Ahram* gives an in-depth English-language coverage of Egyptian and Arabic affairs, the economy, the full spectrum of public opinion, culture and literature, entertainment and weekend travel.

Egypt's state-owned TV channels transmit mainly in Arabic, but with some foreign programmes and films with Arabic subtitles. Channel Two offers a news bulletin in English at 8 p.m. Most of the top-category hotels feature satellite TV, opening up the usual range of programmes courtesy of BBC, CNN and continental stations.

A European radio programme operates on FM 95, with regular news bulletins in most European languages. Check the *Egyptian Gazette* for the day's exact timings of broadcasts in English.

If your holiday would be ruined without important home news like up-to-date Test Match scores, it's worth travelling with a short-wave radio, to pick up the regular on-the-hour news bulletins of the BBC World Service. Reception varies according to time and location, and can always be improved if you take a length of aerial wire to dangle from your hotel window. Try the following wave-lengths:

In northern Egypt: 1323 kHz or 639 kHz on medium wave.

In southern Egypt:

Early morning — 9410 kHz on 31-metre band; 12095 kHz on 25m band; 21470 on 13m.

Day-time — 15070 kHz on 19m band; 17640 on 16m band; 21470 on 13m.

Evening — 9410 kHz on 31-metre band; 15070 on 19m band. 12095 kHz on 25m band; 7325 on 41m band.

Tipping

Tipping is customary for any kind of service, however small. This is a way of life in Egypt. Be tolerant of this habit and don't let it upset you too much. Salaries are low, and *baksheesh* is regarded as a legitimate means of supplementing income. A porter will expect about 50 piastres per bag. If service is not included, a waiter is usually tipped 10%. If a service charge *is* included, an additional 5% is normal.

Ask your tour rep to recommend a suitable scale of tipping. As a typical guideline, think of LE 10 per week for a hotel chambermaid or room boy; LE 2 or 3 for a whole-day sightseeing guide; half that for the driver.

At most museums and archaeological sites, attendants discreetly hold out their hand, and hope.

If they have done nothing but stand there, ignore the outstretched hand. But often they perform some minimal service, like pointing out a showcase or leading you into a temple side-chapel. That's when a 25-piastre banknote comes useful.

To the Western visitor, the constant whisper of *baksheesh, baksheesh* becomes an irritation. It's a good idea to carry plenty of small change, preferably in a baksheesh pocket where otherwise the sight of larger banknotes could inspire more frenzied demands. A good supply of small banknotes is likewise useful in dealing with street vendors, who often profess to have no change when you have handed over a slightly larger note.

Some people take sweets or ball-point pens to give to the local children. Other people discourage the idea, on the grounds that it creates false standards in the young. Egyptian schools are teaching that children should not regard begging as a potential career.

In fact, begging is far less a problem than in former times. There's much more begging in London than in Luxor.

Guides

Official licensed guides adhere to a fixed tariff, set by the local tourist office. Those used by tour operators are excellent linguists, and mostly have spent several university years in ancient Egyptian studies. They can bring every feature of temples and tombs to fascinating life — far better than trudging around independently with a guidebook, however detailed.

However, in all tourist locations you'll be accosted by charming youths or schoolkids who want to practise English, and offer to show you around. These would-be guides usually expect to be paid, even if they offer their services as a friendly gesture. Their expectations — like their expertise — are often greatly over-rated. Most self-appointed guides can do little more than just point to a site, and perhaps tell you its name. No more basic details can be expected. If you *do* wish to be led around, fix a modest price first.

Sexual harassment

Just like in other Mediterranean countries, young bloods fancy themselves as wolves in sheikh's clothing. Many are convinced that unaccompanied foreign females have come solely because of Arab reputation for sexual prowess. They don't want to leave anyone disappointed, and approach anyone who seems likely game.

In crowded locations, foreign women are liable to be petted and pawed. It's an irritation, like mosquitoes, but not threatening. Just ignore it, or snarl. Avoid eye contact. Otherwise, say "NO!" in loud English. Better to stay in a group, and avoid 'provocative' clothing when in public places.

Muslim Holidays

These vary according to the Hegira religious calendar, and move forward by 10 or 11 days each year. There are also numerous local folk festivals called **Moulids**. Although Nubian and Arabic festivals are quite different, all Egyptians unite in celebrating major traditional festivals:

Three days of **Eid al-Fitr**, when all children get handouts of candy, and visits are made to friends and relatives. It marks the end of Ramadan.

Three days of **Eid al-Adha** or **Corban Bairam** — Sacrifice Feast. This is the nearest Muslim equivalent to Christmas, with great slaughter of sheep, generosity to the poor, and postal services clogged with greeting cards. It commemorates the willingness of Abraham — Ibrahim — to sacrifice his son.

Watch these dates! On both these holidays, Egypt closes down on the previous afternoon, with banks and offices shut for the duration. The business visitor will be wasting his time, while the tourist will find transport clogged, and money exchange difficult. Just imagine it's like Christmas in midsummer!

Three weeks after Eid al-Adha is **Ras el-Sana el-Hejira**, which marks New Year's Day in the Muslim calendar.

Moulid al-Nabi, the birthday of the Prophet Mohammed, is marked by many religious processions.

The key dates for 1997 are:

Jan 10 to Feb 9 — Ramadan
Feb 8/11 — 1st Bairam
Apr 20 — Eid al-Adha
May 8 — Hejeri New Year
Jul 17 — Moulid al-Nabi

For 1998, the precise dates will not be announced until near the end of June 1997. If you need them, phone the Islamic Cultural Centre on 0171-724 3363.

Ramadan itself is a month of daytime fasting for the faithful — no food, drink or cigarette smoking between dawn and sunset. Everyone tucks in to a hearty breakfast before sunrise. During daytime, restaurants are virtually empty until the muezzin, TV and radio proclaim the official moment of sunset. Then, instantly, restaurants are suddenly crowded, bursting into cheerful life. Non-Muslims are exempt from fasting, but it's tactful not to smoke in public.

Secular Holidays

Offices and banks will be closed on these days.

Jan 1 — New Year's Day
Apr 25 — Sinai Liberation Day

May 1 — Labour Day
Jul 23 — Anniversary of the 1952 Revolution
Oct 6 — Army Forces Day
Oct 24 — Suez Canal Liberation Day
Dec 23 — Victory Day

Useful Addresses

Egyptian State Tourist Office — 168 Piccadilly, London W1V 9DE Tel: (0171) 493 5282; Fax: (0171) 408 0295

Egyptian Embassy — 26 South Street, London W1Y 9DE Tel: (0171) 499 2401

Egyptian Consulate — 2 Lowndes Street, London SW1X 9ET
Tel: (0171) 235 9777; Visa enquiries: (0171) 235 9719

British Embassy — 7 Ahmed Raghab Street, Garden City, Cairo. Tel: (00 20-2) 354 0890

1.3 Go shopping

Anyone who enjoys hunting for bargains will find endless opportunities. Despite inflation levels which are horrid for the locals, the floating exchange rate helps compensate for the hard-currency visitor. Virtually any locally-produced goods are cheap by West-European standards. On the other hand, because of high import duties, foreign goods are expensive.

Hence the standard rule: don't waste time in looking for non-Egyptian bargains. There aren't any! Indeed, before travelling, be sure to pack adequate supplies of your favourite camera films, suntan lotions, medicaments and toiletries — though, in fact, some of these items are locally manufactured in Egypt under licence.

Where and when to haggle

In the bazaars, fixed prices are a joke, especially for all tourist purchases, including leather goods, antiques and jewellery. All these prices are negotiable. Elsewhere, in Western-style stores, the marked prices are fixed.

To give yourself best chance in a haggling situation, avoid entering any shop 'recommended' by ever-so-friendly characters who engage you in conversation as you wander. The foreign tourist is a potential source of income, a mini gold-mine to be worked by anyone who finds you. A taxi driver will whirl you off on a sightseeing tour, with stops to see his uncle who happens to own a store. Or a street boy — wanting to practise English — will become your self-appointed guide, beating off any rival who tries to take over his pot of gold. Sometimes it's hard to shake them off. The shopkeeper knows that your friendly tout will expect his commission after any sale is made. In turn, this means that your own bargaining power is limited.

Choose your own stores, and make it clear that you are 'shopping around'. If the price is negotiable, it will start crumbling — especially if you can mention that you've seen the same product elsewhere at a much lower price. For any serious purchase, play it the Oriental way. The haggling game should be played with good humour, so that both buyer and seller are happy with the final price. Bartering can be fun, just one part of an Egyptian holiday.

Two of you, shopping together, can try a little play-acting. One can act as the non-buyer offering 'advice' — "It will be cheaper in Luxor/Aswan or wherever," "We don't want that stuff cluttering up the house," or "You know we can't afford it!"

You'll be surprised how quickly the price comes down, somewhat closer to what locals might pay. Don't feel bad about pushing a hard bargain, even if the salesman tells you he has ten hungry children to support. Whatever price you finally agree, it will still be more than a local Egyptian would pay.

Sometimes it can be difficult to gauge a realistic price. If your counter offer is too low, the trader may be offended and not wish to sell. If that happens, just move on. There's always someone else with a similar product.

Most shops are open 9 a.m. till 1 p.m., and re-open 4-8 p.m. They operate a six-day week, closed Friday for midday prayers — though some remain open all seven days. Little corner shops — grocers, greengrocers and the nut and dried-fruit shops — often stay open even later. Post Offices are open daily except Fridays from 9.00 a.m — 2.00 p.m.

Around any tourist-site location, you'll meet persistent salesmanship from a swarm of peddlers. If you're in the market for variegated souvenirs, from postcards to violins with only one string, be prepared with small change. If larger notes are tendered, hawkers often have big problems in finding change — especially when you're buying on the run, with the tour coach ready to leave any moment.

Many Western visitors prefer to buy from possibly more expensive shops, where the sales pressure is less intense, but with fixed prices.

What are the best buys?

Good buys include Egyptian cotton clothes, alabaster, carpets, jewellery, copper utensils, inlaid wooden boxes and chess sets, leather goods and papyrus prints.

Arts and Crafts

The traditions of hand workmanship still flourish in Egypt. Although many souvenirs are specially made for the tourist market on a production line, shoppers can find wide choice of decorative giftware.

There is gleaming copper everywhere. How about a set of the tiny metal pots for making authentic Turkish coffee?

Ceramics are always a popular purchase — particularly tiles and plates, decorated in traditional patterns and colours.

With children in mind, entire caravans of woolly camels are on parade; or the same, carved in wood.

Gold and silver

People sometimes say that gold and silver are 'cheap' in Egypt. In fact, the price of the metal is the same as anywhere else. But Egypt has a major advantage in the relatively low cost of skilled craftsmanship which converts gold into jewellery. In the bazaars, entire sections glisten. Both gold and silver make excellent purchases. Specially popular are the cartouches which can be inscribed with your own name in authentic hieroglyphics.

Be careful where you buy, as the price and more importantly the quality can vary. Always check the hallmark. To help you compare prices, look at page two of *The Egyptian Gazette*, which quotes the day's gold prices in Egyptian pounds per gramme, from 24 carat down to 14. Open negotiations by asking the jeweller his price per gramme for 18-carat, to give a clue on what's being charged for workmanship and general profit margin. All gold items can be priced by weight.

Papyrus

An ideal souvenir, easy to pack and lightweight. Many shops display art-work on papyrus, and can give an interesting talk on how papyrus is made. They'll also explain how to tell 'real' papyrus from the factory product made from banana leaves, and sold by vendors who lurk around tourist sites. Real papyrus can be rolled or folded without damage. The banana-leaf version will crack. If in doubt, ask the sales person if you may bend the corner, just to check.

Inlaid work

Simple but well-made wooden boxes are converted by days of hand craftsmanship into jewellery boxes with exquisite inlaid mother-of-pearl. There are cheap factory-made imitations on the market, which look good until you make a direct comparison with a high-quality product. Hold the box to a light, and check whether the mother-of-pearl colours glisten the way they should.

Alabaster

Can be hand worked or machine made. The widest choice is on the West Bank of Luxor, where many workshops are located. The quality and colour varies. Many shops are crammed with alabaster, turned or carved in every possible shape: vases, egg cups, bowls, ash trays, chess sets.

Carpets

Carpets and rugs are great buys if you really know your subject, and have a clear idea of the equivalent price levels back home. Costs vary greatly, depending on quality which can be difficult for the layman to judge. Most carpets are hand made and are valued by the number of knots per square metre. The most expensive carpets are silk.

Hard bargaining is essential, as opening prices for tourists are outrageous.

1.4 Pickpockets

Just like in any European country, Egypt's main cities have their quota of hardworking pickpockets who specialise in the tourist traffic. Their guess is that holidaymaker handbags or wallets will contain an above-average supply of currency, travellers cheques and credit cards. It's sensible not to travel to Egypt with valued jewellery.

Be careful in crowded places. Pickpockets frequently work in pairs, taking advantage of crowds to jostle or distract their victims while stealing a purse or wallet. A favourite ploy is to draw your attention to a splash of grease on your clothing, and help you clean it off. In the process they also clean up your pockets.

There's no need to go overboard with suspicion of all strangers. But it's sensible not to make things easy for crooks. **Keep handbags fastened and held securely, preferably under your arm. Never carry a wallet in your hip pocket.**

Minimise any potential loss by leaving most of your valuables in the safe deposits available to hotel guests. Keep a separate record of travellers-cheque numbers, and also of where to notify in case of credit-card loss. It's also worth having a photo-copy of your passport details.

If you have anything stolen, make a report to the nearest police station and obtain an official declaration of theft, required for insurance reclaim. If you're on a package tour with insurance cover, contact the travel-agency rep for advice on making a 'Loss Report' to send with your claim form.

Despite these notes of caution, let's emphasise that Egypt has a remarkably low crime rate. Theft is not prevalent. Contrary to general views, Egypt is a very safe country, and the friendly hospitality is unbelievable. Walking at night is perfectly safe around hotels and central areas. In the main tourist locations there are always some tourist police around, and the dice are heavily loaded against any would-be thieves.

Incidentally, tourist police are armed and have a strong presence in Luxor. When visitors first arrive, they are often concerned to see so many guns on the street. This is purely a precautionary measure, to deter any fundamentalists who may want to de-stabilize the tourist industry on which the local people depend so heavily.

Finally, never feel intimidated or obliged to buy anything from street hustlers. They can pester tourists, but are not aggressive.

1.5 Photo hints

In the brilliant Egyptian sunshine, slowish films around ASA 100 will give good results for colour prints. Concentrate your picture-making on early to mid-morning or mid- to late-afternoon. Midday sun gives too much glare, though a lens hood and a polarization filter can help overcome the problem. Towards evening, dusk is of short duration. Capture that sunset picture quickly, before it disappears!

Dust on the lens can be a nuisance. Keep the lens cap in place, whenever the camera is not in use. Bring some lens-cleaning tissue and a dust brush. To protect the lens, it's worth leaving a skylight filter permanently in place — much less costly to renew if over-vigorous cleaning of dust causes scratches.

In the principal tourist locations, local people are accustomed to tourists with their desire to point cameras in every direction. Elsewhere, country folk are less tolerant of any invasion of their privacy. In a similar way, most Brits would be angry if Japanese tourists pointed cameras over the garden gate or into a half-open door.

However, if you don't make a big production of it, you can still get colourful shots of Egyptians in characteristic dress. Position yourself by a monument or in a crowded market. With a wide-angle lens for close-up, or long-focus lens for more distant shots, you can discreetly get all your pictures without irritating anyone. Most camel-drivers and similar characters expect baksheesh if you take their pictures.

In craft workshops, open to tourists, photography is usually OK if you ask permission. Take flash for difficult light conditions in the bazaars. You'll also need it for folklore shows and belly-dancers.

Incidentally, don't waste flash on pictures at Sound & Light performances. There's no way that a modest flash-gun can add anything significant to the lighting of an entire pyramid or temple. If you can find a steady base, or use a tripod, a time exposure will give better chance of success.

Film prices are elastic, depending where you buy. But they shouldn't cost any more than in Britain or USA. However, still take plenty. If you use a specialised film, rather than standard brands, then take an over-supply. Off-beat films are hard to find. Even the favourite international films may not be available when you run out.

Excellent locally-made videos are available at many sites and museums. Several monuments forbid photography, while many museums make a charge for using camera or video equipment. Keep a note of photos taken, and their sequence. Otherwise, back home, it's very difficult to identify every picture.

Pack a light cassette recorder, and capture those evocative Egyptian sounds: the call of the muezzin at 4.30 a.m.; the beating of drums at a folklore show; the grunting of a camel and the screams of its passenger.

1.6 What will the weather be like?

Very hot and dry during the day, except for the winter months of December, January and February when temperatures around Cairo can be a little nippy. Be prepared for cooler nights, even in mid-summer. You'll notice the difference, for instance, when sitting outdoors for a Sound & Light show.

With negligible rainfall, humidity is very low. So even the high daytime temperatures between May and September can be bearable, helped by cool breezes from the river. The main hotels, restaurants and luxury river boats are well equipped with air conditioning.

Occasionally you may meet a sandstorm — unwelcome, though it's guaranteed to make a good conversation piece when you describe the darkening of the sky, the stinging sand, and the wind-heat factor which dries out your throat in minutes.

Remember to take good care of your camera lens — fix the lens cap, and tuck away your camera in a bag as precaution against flying dust and fine sand, which find their way into every little crevice.

TEMPERATURES - Average daily maximum and minimum temperatures - °F.

	J	F	M	A	M	J	J	A	S	O	N	D
CAIRO												
Max	66	69	75	82	90	94	95	96	90	86	75	69
Min	47	49	52	57	63	68	70	69	68	64	58	49
LUXOR												
Max	73	77	84	95	103	105	106	107	101	95	85	77
Min	41	48	52	58	69	73	75	75	70	63	52	47
ASWAN												
Max	75	78	96	95	101	108	106	106	103	98	86	76
Min	50	52	58	64	74	79	79	79	75	71	62	51
AL QUSEIR												
Max	69	70	73	79	85	89	91	92	87	83	78	72
Min	50	54	55	62	70	77	80	81	77	70	60	56
SHARM AL-SHEIKH												
Max	75	78	77	84	91	99	101	100	93	86	82	73
Min	56	57	57	64	75	79	80	79	79	73	66	61

Chapter Two
Cairo

2.1 Invitation to Cairo

For newcomers just in from Europe or America, Cairo can be disconcerting. There are white-robed crowds, noise, rubble, and entire bazaar sections seething with activity. Beat-up buses belch exhaust fumes, and are festooned with out-riding passengers who can't squeeze inside.

The Egyptian capital offers great contrasts. Africa's most vibrant city is often clogged to a standstill with traffic but also is equipped with highspeed elevated highways, tunnels and wide Nile bridges. Luxury hotels and international-style office blocks are built totally in the modern idiom. There are garden suburbs of tree-lined avenues and tranquil public parks.

During a few days in the Egyptian capital, most visitors have time only for the ancient world of Pyramids, Sphinx and the Egyptian Museum: nothing less than 3500 years old. But it's also worth sampling the more modern Cairo which has grown during the last 2,000 years.

The area of Greater Cairo has been settled since prehistory. According to tradition, Old Cairo itself was founded by Babylonian prisoners of war captured by Ramses II in 13th century BC. Hence an earlier name of the city was Babylon-in-Egypt, so called by the Romans and later by the Crusaders. The Islamic name of Cairo — El Qahira, or 'The Victorious' — didn't appear until 969 AD.

The Romans always had a sharp eye for a strategic site. When they took over Egypt in 30 BC, after crushing Cleopatra, they garrisoned a legion on a dominant hilltop where today's Citadel commands a superb viewpoint over the sprawling city.

Part of the Christian story is closely linked to Babylon-in-Egypt. Legend says that Joseph and Mary sought refuge here with infant Jesus. More certain is that Saint Mark arrived in 45 AD on his mission to convert Egypt. According to Coptic tradition, Mark wrote his Gospel here during that period, though the main setting for early Christianity was Alexandria. But, ever since, Old Cairo has remained a major centre for the Christian faith.

Old Cairo is worth visiting for its Coptic Museum and churches, clustered beside Babylon's gateway towers built by the Romans. The Copts claim direct descent from the ancient Egyptians. Their spoken and written language provided the linguistic key that helped de-code the hieroglyphs last century. Coptic manuscripts were written in a modified Greek alphabet, but followed the speech patterns and vocabulary of ancient Egypt.

When triumphant Islam arrived in 640 AD, the Arab conquerors left the Jews and Christians undisturbed in their Coptic enclave of Babylon. The new rulers built an Islamic city just north of Old Cairo, and then spread out over the centuries. Each dynasty for 900 years left a rich heritage of public buildings — mosques, schools, hospitals, city gates and fortifications.

Cairo grew into a major Islamic religious and cultural centre. While Europe was in the Dark Ages, the Mosque of al-Azhar — founded in 970 — became the world's first university, teaching Islamic law and doctrine. A thousand years later, it still thrives, with free lodging for students.

For the short-time visitor, Islamic Cairo is a bewildering maze of narrow alleys, medieval dwellings, bazaars and majestic mosques. A half-day guided tour skims the surface — the Citadel, a couple of mosques, and the Khan el-Khalili bazaar quarter. It would take months to explore its full diversity.

During the past 200 years, Cairo has moved towards Western-style modernization. Since the mid-19th century, Cairo has adopted European styles of city planning, with layout of wide thoroughfares, large squares and park areas. Palaces, museums and other public buildings were set up.

Today's downtown area around Midan Tahrir is typical, with avenues that fan out from the square, and one-way traffic systems. Just south of this central area is the embassy quarter of Garden City. Riverside promenades open up views of the Nile and the islands of Roda and Gezira.

Ever since building of the Suez Canal, Cairo has filled a key position in the great land mass of Europe, Asia and Africa: a land bridge between the continents, and the shortest sea route between Mediterranean and Indian Ocean. Located on the world's longest river, Cairo is the gateway into Africa. The resulting mixture of cultures — African, Middle Eastern and European — have all contributed to the city's vitality.

In Arab society — from Morocco to the Gulf — Cairo is the intellectual and cultural magnet. Its book publishing, music and film industries cater for the entire Arab world. During July and August, every hotel is filled with Arab families on holiday from the Gulf. Cairo is their dream of sophisticated living.

The western visitor can enjoy travelling through time, from one period to another. Pharaohs who died several thousand years ago can still display their personality, with every detail of their daily lives portrayed in tombs or preserved in museums. Past and present meet. When you travel by tour coach to Sakkara and Memphis — Egypt's first-ever capital — you can glimpse a rural life-style that fundamentally has not changed for 5,000 years.

Kilns with tall tower-like chimneys produce bricks, but village houses are still made of mud. In market gardens beside road and river, water is raised by donkey-power, though electric pumps are taking over. Crops include broad beans, tomatoes, potatoes, wheat and maize. Other fields carry rice; or clover for the animals.

Alongside the highway is a separate track for horse- and donkey-carts. Children play in the irrigation canals, and women paddle in to wash clothes. There are grazing camels, sheep, water buffalo, cows and goats. Palm groves offer shade. Dates are harvested around September — a popular fruit when dried, for consumption during Ramadan. Egypt is now the world's largest exporter of dates, having taken over from Iraq. You can enjoy all these country scenes within a 30-minute drive of central Cairo. It's all part of the diversity of Egypt's capital.

2.2 Arrival & hotels

From London Heathrow, daily 4½-hour non-stop flights are operated by EgyptAir (from Terminal 3) and British Airways (Terminal 4). Cairo airport has two terminals, about two miles apart. EgyptAir, the national airline, uses Terminal 1 — the Old Terminal — for all its domestic and international flights. British Airways uses Terminal 2.

If you don't have a pre-arranged travel-agency transfer to your hotel, a cab-ride to central Cairo should cost around LE 25 — say, £5 sterling, though the driver's opening bid will probably start higher. On a night-time arrival, the 14-mile journey from the city's north-east outskirts will take about 30 minutes to downtown. But if you travel the distance during Cairo's rush hour — 8 a.m. till 8 p.m. — reckon twice as long.

The drive into town passes through **Heliopolis** — a grid-pattern garden city which has flowered in the 20th century, taking its name from the Greek, meaning Sun City. It's an upmarket residential area, where many foreign companies base their Cairo offices. The broad central boulevard is called El-Uruba. Starting from the airport hotels, Novotel and Mövenpick, several other international hotel groups are located along the highway: Sheraton, Meridien and Sonesta.

The official residence of the President is sited in this area, to the right, with guards outside. Then left, past the Sonesta Hotel, comes Cairo Stadium and Cairo International Fair. You'll also see a circular building, the October War museum that depicts the October 1973 war between Israel and Egypt.

El-Uruba boulevard converts into Salah Salem Avenue, the longest thoroughfare in Cairo. It by-passes the centre to give speedy access to Old Cairo, Roda Island and thence direct to the Pyramids at the opposite end of town.

Meanwhile the route between Heliopolis and downtown Cairo swings into the 6th of October Skyway — nine miles long — via the Abasiya Flyover, past the Coptic Cathedral of St. Marks. You get a quick glance at the white facade of Ramses main railway station — or, the other side, of a 30-ft statue of Ramses II himself. They are separated by the flyover and 3500 years.

The elevated highway heads towards the skyscraper Hotel Ramses Hilton, and you know that you've arrived. All the central hotels are within a few minutes' drive. The 6th of October expressway continues, bridging the Nile across Gezira Island. Maybe you're wondering where are all those traffic jams you've read about?

2.3 Get your bearings

If you are staying in any of the downtown high-rise hotels beside the Nile, you can start getting clues to orientation by looking out of your bedroom window, or from a roof-top bar or restaurant.

The airport in northeast Cairo is 14 miles from the centre. From the centre to the Pyramids on Cairo's south-west outskirts is another 9 miles. The basic city, 23 miles across, is home to upwards of 15 million people. Slicing through this megapolis, south to north, is the River Nile, which is split by two long **islands** — **Roda** and **Gezira**.

Most of the tourist action is on the east bank of the Nile. Facing the southern tip of Roda Island is the original Old Cairo — the **Coptic Cairo** which the Romans enclosed with a city wall.

North and east of that location lies the heartland of **Islamic Cairo**, settled by successive dynasties up to the **Citadel** walls. That's the area of the great and historic mosques and the bazaar district of **Khan el-Khalili**.

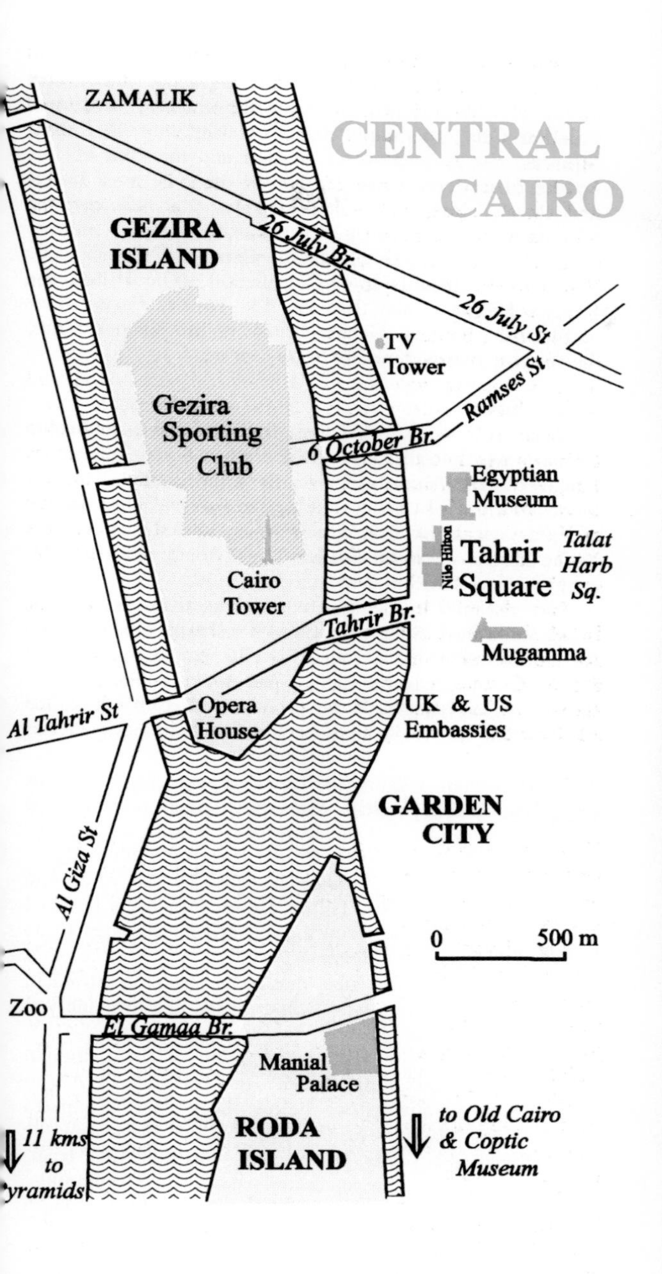
ZAMALIK
CENTRAL
CAIRO
GEZIRA
ISLAND
26 July Br.
26 July St
TV
Tower
Ramses St
Gezira
Sporting
Club
6 October Br.
Egyptian
Museum
Nile Hilton
Tahrir
Square
Talat
Harb
Sq.
Cairo
Tower
Tahrir Br.
Mugamma
Al Tahrir St
Opera
House
UK & US
Embassies
GARDEN
CITY
Al Giza St
0
500 m
Zoo
El Gamaa Br.
Manial
Palace
RODA
ISLAND
11 kms
to
to Old Cairo
& Coptic
Museum

The modern downtown area faces the northern tip of Roda Island, and the southern half of Gezira Island. That sweep of central Cairo embraces the embassy district of **Garden City**, the major transportation hub of **Tahrir Square**; and up to **Ramses Station** and the 26th of July Street. That street continues across the Nile as a bridge and elevated highway to the residential and business area of **Zamalek**, the northern half of Gezira Island.

The tall landmarks of central Cairo are the riverside hotels — Semiramis Inter-Continental, Nile Hilton and Ramses Hilton — and then the **TV Tower**. Facing them across the river on Gezira Island is the slender **Cairo Tower**, topped by a revolving restaurant.

Tahrir Square

Most newcomers to Cairo soon find themselves in **Midan Tahrir**, which translates as Liberation Square. Visitors, however, feel themselves virtually imprisoned by the relentless torrent of traffic. The key to survival is to use the spacious system of underpasses which also act as entrance to the **Metro — Sadat Station**. Look for a red-letter 'M' enclosed in a star and a red circle.

Part reason for the apparent traffic chaos is that the centre of Tahrir Square is Cairo's **central bus terminal** for innumerable routes around the city. At the south end of the huge square is the launch-pad for minibuses, overlooked by an enormous government office block called **Mugamma**, filled with bureaucrats. The building itself was a brotherly gift of the Soviet Union.

Most foreign visitors to Tahrir Square come for the **Egyptian Archaeological Museum**, which occupies the north side of Midan Tahrir. In front is parking for the tour coaches that bring visitors for their museum sightseeing.

Another side of the square is filled by the white and blue complex of the **Nile Hilton Hotel**. Possibly a hundred cabs are parked in the vicinity, with drivers all eager to do business with stray foreigners. *They* hail *you*, not the other way round. You'll also meet numerous souvenir salesmen, and friendly characters who would dearly like to guide you to their favourite shops.

Opposite the Nile Hilton are many of the principal airline offices, including British Airways and TWA (located on the ground floor below the corner Cleopatra Hotel). Road planners of the 19th century chose not the conventional square city grid system, but more of a triangular pattern, like their ancestors who designed pyramids. The resulting geometry means that if you reach Talat Harb Midan or Square, you have choice of six different directions.

Wander at random in that area, where virtually every street is devoted to lower-cost hotels, travel agencies, restaurants, bars and all the shopping — mostly fixed-price — that your feet can handle. When you're totally bushed, just ask your way back to Midan Tahrir, or stop a passing taxi.

2.4 Basic Cairo — the highlights

A standard half-day conducted tour normally includes a visit to the Egyptian Museum, where guides focus on the great highlights including the treasures of Tutankhamun. The tour would then feature the Citadel with its Mosque of Mohammed Ali; and a stroll through the Khan el-Khalili Bazaar.

2.4.1 The Egyptian Antiquities Museum

Founded in 1858 and opened in its present central location on Tahrir Square in 1902, this is Egypt's finest museum, covering 3000 years of Pharaonic history. It houses the world's greatest collection of Egyptian antiquities. In a two- or three-hour visit it's possible to see only a small fraction of the 100,000 exhibits. Unless time is very short, schedule a return visit to look closer at whatever captures your interest on a lightning sightseeing.

Besides the usual ticket price, extra is payable for use of cameras. The museum is open daily 9-17 hrs; but on Fridays from 9-12 and 14-17 hrs, so that the staff can take a break for Friday prayers. The pleasant entrance gardens feature a serene-looking sphinx, sacred baboons, granite pharaohs, and a pool with living papyrus and lotus — the floral symbols of Upper and Lower Egypt.

Inside the museum, exhibits are arranged in date order. If you want to be very thorough, turn left at the entrance, and trudge round a sequence of outer galleries that feature Old, Middle and New Kingdom, and ending with the Greeks and Romans.

A shorter cut is to head straight from the entrance rotunda, through the central Atrium with its highlights from the Dynasties, finishing at the Amarna Gallery in Room 3.

Depending on the crowds, you could zoom directly upstairs to the two wings of Tutankhamun galleries with his coffins, jewellery, arrows, furniture and the much-photographed golden mask. The crowds are normally thickest in Rooms 2, 3 and 4, with their dazzling displays of gold and jewels. Tut's coffin weighs 243 lbs of solid 22-carat gold.

In the furthermost corner of the same floor is Room 56, where eleven royal mummies are once again on display, having been off limits to public view from 1979 till 1993. The showcases are kept under rigid control of oxygen, temperature and humidity levels, to replicate closely the original conditions of their tombs in Luxor's Valley of the Kings.

2.4.2 Islamic Cairo

From 3000 BC, Egyptian civilisation developed to great heights in architecture, sculpture and painting. There were some design changes during Greek and Roman rule. But the arrival of Islam in 640 AD ushered in a totally new era. The power base moved from Alexandria, and Cairo was established as the first Islamic capital of Egypt.

The new rulers brought an entirely different building style which developed under the various dynasties that ruled Egypt — the Omayyads, the Abbasids, the Tulunids, the Fatimids, the Ayyubids, the Mamelukes and, finally, the Ottomans. The city became a great intellectual centre.

To get the flavour, visit one or two of the historic mosques, and explore the narrow streets of the bazaar quarter of Khan el-Khalili.

Just a reminder of mosque etiquette: sober dress; leave shoes at entrance with the attendant who will expect a little baksheesh, or wear 'overshoes' of denim, or carry shoes with you, sole to sole. See page 106 for comments on mosque architecture. Roughly in date order, here's a short list of historic mosques, which mostly charge an entrance fee for non-Muslims.

Amr Mosque

This was Egypt's first-ever mosque, built in 642 AD just north of Coptic Cairo. Its original design was simple. Pillars were palm tree trunks, roofed by palm leaves. Improvements and extensions came over the years, so that none of the original structure remains.

Today's mosque comprises a vast open courtyard surrounded by four loggias, the largest one containing the prayer niche, facing Mecca. Marble columns are in different styles and some of the walls are panelled with wood carvings.

Tulun Mosque

The largest and oldest Mosque to retain its original materials and architectural character. It was built 879 AD by Ibn Tulun, who came from Iraq and founded the Tulunid Dynasty. The red-brick style is derived from the Samarra

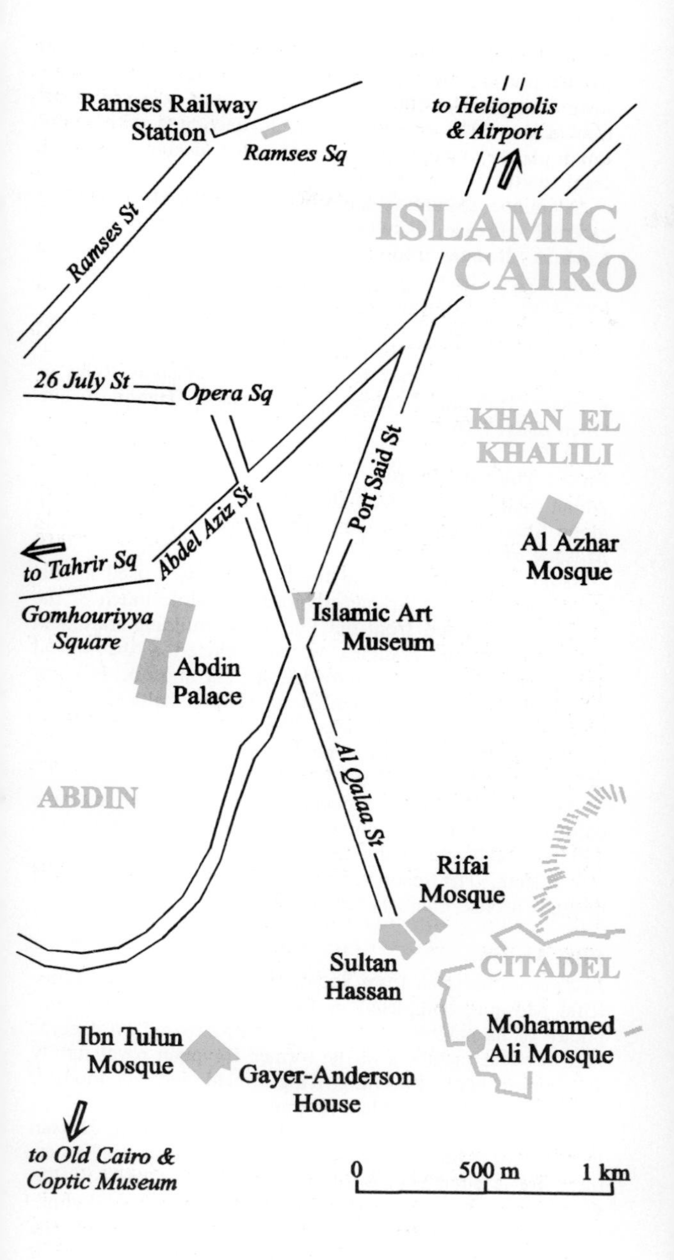
Ramses Railway Station
Ramses Sq
to Heliopolis & Airport
Ramses St
ISLAMIC CAIRO
26 July St
Opera Sq
KHAN EL KHALILI
Port Said St
Abdel Aziz St
to Tahrir Sq
Al Azhar Mosque
Gomhouriyya Square
Islamic Art Museum
Abdin Palace
ABDIN
Al Qalaa St
Rifai Mosque
Sultan Hassan
CITADEL
Mohammed Ali Mosque
Ibn Tulun Mosque
Gayer-Anderson House
to Old Cairo & Coptic Museum
0
500 m
1 km

Mosque near Baghdad where an entire city population met for Friday prayers. Hence the simple design, with a huge open courtyard — 100 yards square — and a central ablution facility. The arcades are richly decorated with sculptured plaster, using vine-leaf and other designs based on Iraqi motifs.

A unique feature is the stone minaret with a winding external staircase, likewise inspired by the great minaret at Samarra. It dates from 1296, replacing the original in the same style. The minaret balcony offers a spectacular view over Cairo with distant Pyramids in hazy outline.

Adjoining Ibn Tulun mosque is the **Gayer-Anderson House**, donated by a British major in 1942 as a twin-mansion museum furnished in a variety of Oriental styles — Persian, Turkish, Chinese. There's also a Harem Room. Open daily 9-16 hrs.

Sultan Hassan Mosque

About half a mile from Ibn Tulun Mosque — heading along Sharia Saliba towards the Citadel — is the splendid Mosque of Sultan Hassan.

Gold and marble of the finest quality was used in this great showpiece of Arabic architecture, while much of the stone was recycled from the Pyramids. Building started in 1356 AD on the complex which included a theological school with student accommodation. The mosque is composed of an open court with four vaulted halls that look onto the domed ablution area. The halls served as lecture rooms for the four law schools of Sunni Islam. On the outside are buildings of the four colleges.

The entire concept is deeply impressive, with massive construction and vast domes. The enormous entrance is 130 feet high and is the finest of its kind among Islamic monuments. The mausoleum of Sultan Hassan is reached through bronze doors behind the mihrab.

Rifai Mosque

Just across the road from Sultan Hassan is the 19th-century Rifai Mosque, completed in 1912. In contrast to the simplicity of its neighbour, no expense was spared on decoration. Several members of the former Egyptian royal family are buried here, including King Fouad and his mother, together with the last Shah of Iran.

Steps between the mosques of Rifai and Sultan Hassan lead up into Midan Salah Al-Din — Saladin Square. Pause there for a superb view of the crenellated Citadel walls, with towers and minarets silhouetted against the skyline. Keep left of the walls, uphill all the way, to reach the Citadel's main entrance. En route you'll see the typical side streets and alleys of a Cairo which has changed little since medieval days.

Al Azhar Mosque

Finally, in this brief listing of Cairo's principal mosques, let's mention Al Azhar which is located by the bazaar area of Khan El Khalili, and reached by an underpass below Al Azhar Square. Founded in 972 AD, it doubles as the world's oldest university. For over a thousand years it has given a classic Islamic education free to Muslim students of all nationalities.

As a major religious centre, it was also a centre of 19th-century nationalism. Politically it has played a role in more recent history. It was the setting for a belligerent speech by Nasser during the Suez crisis of 1956. It's worth climbing to the roof, or up the minaret, for another view over medieval Cairo.

2.4.3 The Citadel

When Richard the Lionheart led Crusaders in the Holy Land, his chivalrous opponent was Saladin, the warrior Sultan of Egypt. During Saladin's reign — 1171 to 1193 — he developed Cairo's fortifications in defence against potential Crusader attack. Building of the Citadel began in 1176 AD, using the pyramids as a stone quarry.

The medieval fortress was greatly extended in later years. Saladin's nephew established the Citadel as a royal residence. During Sultan al-Nasir's reign, some existing buildings were replaced by palaces. The **Mosque of Sultan al-Nasir** was completed by 1335, with a Persian touch to the corkscrew minarets and the dome.

The present-day Citadel is linked mainly with Mohammed Ali, the Ottoman pasha who turned Egypt around during the early 19th century. He organised a post-banquet massacre of 470 members of the Mameluke aristocracy, and built a mosque which dominates the Cairo skyline.

Mosque of Mohammed Ali

Also known as the **Marble Mosque**, the interior is decorated in the most grandiose Ottoman style, inspired by the big mosques of Istanbul — dome architecture gone mad. The mosque was completed in 1848. Mohammed Ali died insane the following year, and is buried here in a white marble tomb.

The clock in the ablutions courtyard was presented by Louis Philippe of France, but it regrettably has never worked. The timepiece was a straight swap for the obelisk in Place de la Concorde in Paris.

Behind the Mohammed Ali Mosque is a terrace which gives a commanding view over Cairo, and especially down to the Sultan Hassan and Rifai Mosques.

There are several other points of interest within the Citadel grounds: everything kept in very trim condition, with manicured lawns, greenery, plants and trees.

The **Police National Museum** features a display of cells through the centuries, murders and assassinations. The **Military Museum** exhibits army relics, uniforms and hardware from ancient Egyptian times to the tank age. The **Mosque of Suleyman Pasha** was built in 1528, after the Ottomans took power. **Yussuf's Well** was dug by Crusader prisoners during Saladin's time, over 300 feet down, to ensure water supplies in case of seige. **Al Gawhara Palace** was built by Mohammed Ali to house his harem, and is now a jewellery museum. The **Carriage Museum** features royal carriages, coachmen's livery, horse saddles and paintings. The Citadel is open daily 9-17 hrs.

2.4.4 Old Cairo (Babylon-in-Egypt)

In contrast to the bedlam of central Cairo, the Coptic Museum area offers total tranquillity, only four Metro stops from the hubbub of Tahrir Square. As you emerge from **Mari Girgis** station, the entrance to the Coptic Museum is right there. Mari Girgis means Saint George — the name of the circular church facing the remains of a circular Roman tower.

The **Roman fortress** was built by Emperor Augustus in 30 AD, alongside the Nile which has since changed course, moving about 400 yards west. Most of the Coptic churches were built within the fortress walls, which defied the invading Arabs for seven months in 640 AD.

With the Arabs settling north of Old Cairo, half a dozen of these Coptic churches have survived the centuries, and are tightly clustered in the area. They are among the oldest churches in the world. Christian Egypt is still present and alive in its ancient remains and modern sanctuaries. It is the link between Pharaonic civilisation and the more recent Islamic age. The word 'Copt' derives from the Greek *Aiguptios*, meaning Egyptian.

Coptic Museum

The museum contains the world's largest collection of Coptic remains, mainly covering the period from 3rd to 7th century. It is one of the four major museums (the others being the Egyptian and Islamic Museums in Cairo and the Greco-Roman Museum in Alexandria) which cover the whole span of Egyptian history.

On the ground floor are sculptures, bronzes and woodcarvings from earliest Christian times. On the floor above are manuscripts, textiles and vividly painted icons. The manuscripts are on both papyrus and parchment — the latter made from the skins of gazelles. Some of the texts are bilingual, in Greek and Coptic; others are in Arabic and Coptic. These documents are a joy to scholars, for whom Coptic is a bridge to the language and hieroglyphs of ancient Egypt.

The Coptic Museum was formerly a palace. Quite apart from all the Coptic relics, look at the beautifully carved ceilings: all different, no pattern repeated. The wooden lattice screens on the windows are likewise masterpieces of traditional carving.

Open daily 9-16 hrs. Tel: 841766.

Ben Ezra Synagogue
The former Jewish community has dwindled away, with a 20th-century exodus to Israel. For the few remaining families, occasional services are held in the Ben Ezra Synagogue, which is part of the Old Cairo complex. The synagogue was built in the 9th century on the site of the 4th-century St. Michael's church which the Christians sold to pay taxes that helped finance building of the Ibn Tulun mosque.

Within walking distance, northwards, is **Amr Mosque** — the first of the Islamic era. See page 34.

2.4.5 The Nile Islands

As the Nile flows northwards with Cairo on the right bank and Ghizeh on the left, the two long islands of Roda and Gezira offer a more spacious residential life-style. Buildings on the two islands are almost entirely 20th-century, as they were exposed to Nile flooding until construction of the first Aswan Dam in 1902. Bridges carry a heavy flow of cross-river traffic. But elevated and multi-lane highways avoid the calmer tree-lined streets of the residential sectors. Several excellent hotels are located in peaceful island settings. But downtown Cairo is only a few minutes' distance from Gezira; or Garden City and Coptic Cairo from Roda.

Gezira Island
The southern half of Gezira is particularly green with parks and the exclusive **Gezira Sporting Club**. The Club grounds were a British Army enclave, especially where cavalry officers played polo. The club and its race-course

were also open to the diplomatic corps and to suitably well-born Egyptians. In today's republic, membership is restricted by high membership fees.

The northern end of Gezira is **Zamalek** — a high-grade area of elegant villas and apartments, embassies, foreign banks and offices.

Cairo Tower

Gezira's most prominent landmark is Cairo Tower. Built in 1961 with Soviet help, it stands over 600 feet high and commands magnificent views across the city. After visiting the 16th floor viewing level, you can take light refreshments in the café on the 15th floor. There is also a revolving restaurant on the 14th floor.

Open daily from 9 a.m. till midnight. Entry is LE 14.

Egyptian Civilization Museum

In the Gezira Exhibition Grounds, Agricultural Society Pavilion. Collections of paintings and sculptures that reflect the entire history of Egypt from prehistoric times till the present. This museum has been closed for renovation. Phone 340-5198 to check whether it has yet reopened.

Cairo Opera House

This ultra-modern complex for the performing arts is located by el-Tahrir Street on the southern end of Gezira. As a gift from the Japanese, the Opera House combines traditional Islamic motifs with elements of the Orient and the West — the work of a Japanese architect. The building replaces a former Opera House which was burnt down during 1971 riots.

Check current programmes for western-style opera, ballet, symphonic and chamber music; and also performances of Arabic music and dance. Touring groups add to the international cultural flavour.

Dress: jacket and tie. Tel: 342-0603.

Egyptian Modern Art Museum

Another new public building, close to the Opera House, showing works by 20th-century Egyptian and foreign artists.

Open 10-13 hrs and 17-21.30 hrs. Closed Mon. Tel: 341-6665. Entrance free.

Mahmoud Khalil Museum

Located in Zamalek district, next to Cairo Marriott Hotel, and opposite the entrance to the Gezira Sporting Club. A superb private collection was formed by a wealthy young man who studied in Paris during the early 20th century.

Enthused by art, he started to buy Impressionist paintings, and continued for some 30 years to acquire works by Pissarro, Toulouse Lautrec, Monet, Corot, van Gogh and Gauguin. The museum also displays several Rodin sculptures, and Islamic and Far Eastern artefacts. The building was a former royal residence of a cousin to King Fouad.

Open daily except Fri 10-14 hrs. Tel: 341-8672.

The Centre of Arts

Three art galleries are housed in a former palace in the Zamalek district of Gezira Island. See local English-language press for details of exhibitions.

Open daily 9-13 and 17-20 hrs. Tel: 340-8211.

Roda Island

From the 13th to 18th centuries, Roda was a fortified island with army barracks, sultan palaces and mosques. Then it fell into virtual disuse until the 20th century.

Manial Palace Museum

Located on Sayala Street close to Cairo University Bridge. It was built 1903 in medieval fortress style for Prince Mohammed Ali Tewfik, cousin of King Farouk. It features architectural styles from Morocco, Persia, Turkey and Egypt. On view are rare carpets, textiles, precious stones and hunting trophies. The beautiful and spacious garden, filled with exotic tropical plants, is shared with the Manial Palace Hotel. Open daily 9-16 hrs. Tel: 987495.

The Nilometer

At the southern tip of Roda Island, the Nilometer was built in 861 AD to measure the river's water level, and hence to estimate the potential harvest in the Delta. Stairs lead to the bottom of a square well. In the middle, a marble column is marked to indicate water heights. The pointed arches are the first of their kind in Egyptian Islamic architecture. The cone-shaped roof was added last century.

Entrance LE 6, plus a tip to the keeper.

Dr. Ragab's Pharaonic Village

Most of Jacob's Island — just south of Roda Island — has been converted into a living model of ancient Egyptian life. You float by a replica temple with its sacred lake, a nobleman's villa and a peasant's house. A hundred performers re-enact typical daily activities. There's also a reproduction of Tutankhamun's tomb, including the antechamber, the burial chamber and the treasury room with layout of the contents as discovered in 1922. The two-hour tour costs LE 40. Open daily 9-16 hrs. Tel: 629266.

2.5 Other sights and museums

Dr. Fagab's Papyrus Institute

This floating 'institute' is permanently docked on the Giza side of the river, south of Cairo Sheraton Hotel. Dr. Hassan Fagab — a former ambassador — set up this museum to display all aspects of the papyrus-making process. Papyrus reproductions are sold of ancient Egyptian paintings. Art exhibitions are held regularly.

Open daily 10-19 hrs. Tel: 348-8676.

Railway Museum

A joy for train fans, this museum is part of the Ramses Railway Station on Ramses Square. It features an automated display of trains and railway coaches, including Khedive Ismail's private train. Open daily except Mon 9-14 hrs.

All true train lovers should travel there by Metro — three stops from Sadat Station on Tahrir Square to Mubarak, which is the stop for Ramses main station. Don't forget to inspect the statue of Ramses II on the square outside. The 30-ft statue in red granite was moved here from Memphis in 1955.

Islamic Art Museum

Located in Port Said Street on Ahmad Maher Square, it shares the same building as the national public library. The museum contains the world's largest and rarest collection of Muslim art through the ages, and includes tapestries, ceramics, carved wood, metalwork, illustrated Korans and glass mosque lamps.

There are architectural panels of carved marble or wood from palaces and mosques. The 75,000 items present a full picture of Islamic art and civilisation and include exhibits from Persia, Turkey and Egypt.

Open daily 9-16 hrs. Tel: 903930. Entrance LE 16.

Abdin Palace

Building of this European-style luxury palace in the 1860's was among the projects which virtually bankrupted 19th-century Egypt. It became the centre of government and was the official residence of King Farouk until his exile in 1952. It functions today as the president's state headquarters.

The palace is located on Gomhouriyya Square (which means Republic Square) in the Abdin quarter of Cairo — fairly close to the Islamic Art Museum mentioned above.

October War Panorama
Near the HQ of Egypt's military establishment, this circular museum building is sited by the corner of El-Uruba and Ismail el-Fangary Streets in Heliopolis. It depicts the war of October 1973 when Egyptian forces crossed the Suez Canal during the Israeli Yom Kippur holiday, and attacked the Bar-Lev Line. A panoramic battle scene shows the Egyptian capture of the canal town of Qantara.

Open daily except Tue. Check first on times of audio-visual shows, which normally are in Arabic. Tel: 602317.

2.6 The Giza Pyramids

These massive monuments of the Pharaohs on the desert outskirts of Cairo are the only survivors of the Seven Wonders of the Ancient World. The big three were built for Cheops, his son Chephren, and grandson Mycerinus — all within a single century.

Experts calculate that the 450-ft high **Great Pyramid of Cheops** (also known as Khufu, who lived around 2550 BC) required 20 years' labour to erect the 2.5 million limestone blocks. The Greek writer Heredotus said over 100,000 men were employed on the task, but the number is suspect. Anyway he can hardly be accepted as a contemporary observer. In mid-5th century BC, he was writing 2,000 years after the Pyramids were built.

During the annual Nile flood, when fields were deep below water, the Pharaoh set his subjects to work on these projects that aimed to ensure eternal life for the king when he died. It *wasn't* slave labour, but a kind of national service: workfare with free food. These big projects kept agricultural labourers out of mischief while they waited 100 days each year for the river to subside. Possibly up to 50,000 men sweated on all the ancillary tasks of quarrying, river transport, and hauling stone blocks to the work-site. In addition, an elite work-force of skilled masons, artisans and craftsmen was employed year-round.

Apart from all these vital statistics or numerical guesses, the Pyramids still arouse wonder at the high-tech civil engineering that went into their construction. All the Pyramids were precisely oriented to the Polar Star of 4,500 years ago, with equally precise right-angles at each corner. Construction had to be dead level at every stage, to ensure that the pyramid didn't end up skewed.

Despite great ingenuity to foil access to the burial chambers, tomb robbers cleaned out the treasures many centuries ago. Present-day visitors walk crouching up duck boards along an uphill shaft, which is not recommended

Pyramids of Giza

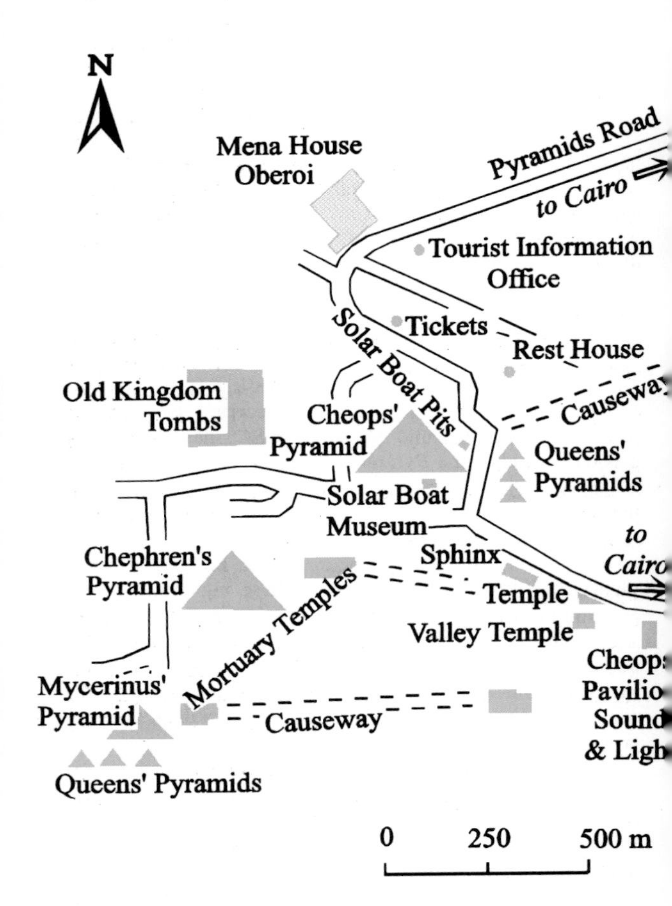

for claustrophobes or professional basketball players. Guides try to shuffle their itineraries, to avoid having too many tour groups milling up and down simultaneously.

Close to the eastern flank of the Pyramid of Cheops lie three small pyramids dedicated to his wives.

Pyramid of King Chephren

Cheops' son was Chephren, who built his own pyramid south-west of dad's, but a respectful ten feet lower in height. In the upper levels, it still shows remnants of the limestone casing that once covered it entirely. The interior is simple, with two entrances on the north side.

Due east, facing the dawn sun, are remains of Chephren's mortuary temple, where priests would make offerings to ensure that the king would have a good afterlife and ultimate resurrection. From there, a 450-yard causeway leads down to the Valley Temple of Chephren, built of limestone faced with Aswan granite. This temple was likewise dedicated to religious rites for the dead king.

The Sphinx

Close to the Valley Temple lies the enormous Sphinx — one of the world's most recognizable monuments. Shaped from a huge outcrop of limestone, this legendary statue has the body of a lion and the face of a man, symbolic of strength and wisdom. Scholars guess it was modelled on King Chephren. He's showing signs of old age, with a crumbling surface and the removal of his beard to the British Museum. The missing nose is blamed on 14th-century artillery practice.

Pyramid of Mycerinus

Completing the trio of king-sized pyramids is the more modest Pyramid of Mycerinus, who ruled 2490-2472 BC as the successor of Chephren. Only 200 feet high, it stands south-west of the Cheops and Chephren pyramids. Its lower levels still retain their original granite slab coverings.

The three pyramids of Giza are surrounded by several small pyramids, and hundreds of Mastaba-tombs of lesser royals, nobles, priests and other VIP's.

The Solar Boat

The ancient Egyptians carved large pits in the rock, near the pyramids. There they placed wooden boats, to be ready and waiting for the king when he went on his journey of day and night with the sun god, Ra.

Excavations have discovered three sun boat sites close to the Great Pyramid. The pit uncovered in 1954 was roofed with massive limestone slabs, hermetically sealed so that even insects were excluded. Entombed in the pit was a complete 140-ft boat made of Lebanese cedar.

After years of dedicated restoration, the vessel is housed in a purpose-built air-conditioned museum by the south side of Cheops' pyramid. The craft can rightly be claimed as the world's oldest surviving boat - giving an insight into the grandeur of the Pharaohs' life-style.

The museum outlines how the find was made; a view of the pit itself, with 18-ton limestone blocks still in place; and showcases that give a close-up sample of the original knotted papyrus ropes that lashed the boat timbers together. No nails were used.

The boat itself is supremely graceful, with not a clumsy line anywhere. The Solar Boat was not solar-powered! It needed a crew of 25, with two men on each oar, five oars on each side.

A photography permit is required, in addition to the entrance fee. Full excavation of another solar boat pit must wait until funds are available.

The classic view

A neighbouring hill offers a classic panorama of the three main pyramids, with foreground camels, horses and occasional donkeys. Chaps on camel-back are eager to pose for you, like film extras against a background of the pyramids. They are quick to spot anyone who lines them up for a photo, and baksheesh is expected.

2.7 Memphis and Sakkara

About 20 miles south of central Cairo, near the left bank of the Nile, is the ancient site of Memphis, founded around 3100 BC by Menes, the first king of the 1st Dynasty.

As the foundation capital of the Old Kingdom, Memphis kept its importance for many centuries, with major ceremonies held to mark coronations and jubilee festivals. But little remains today of the original magnificence. The mud bricks of 5,000 years ago have oozed back into the overlying Nile silt.

Only Ramses II (13th century BC) has left his mark with the remains of a huge fallen limestone statue, now sheltered under concrete. In the adjoining garden is a varied collection of monuments, including a superb 80-ton alabaster Sphinx.

Much more permanent were the burial arrangements for royalty, nobles and priests in neighbouring Sakkara. The desert hilltop location overlooking Memphis was safely beyond the reach of the Nile floods.

This vast necropolis — four miles north to south; one mile east to west — is dominated by the famous Step Pyramid, designed as the burial place of King Zoser of the Third Dynasty. Dating from about 2700 BC, this 204-ft-high construction is Egypt's first pyramid, and ranks as the oldest stone structure of that size in the world.

The Step Pyramid is the centrepiece of a complex enclosed within a mile of walls. There's a colonnaded corridor from the entrance gateway, a Mortuary Chapel, and a replica of court buildings to provide a suitable setting for ceremonies in the after-life.

Smaller pyramids are located in the area — all somewhat dwarfed by the Step Pyramid of Zoser. Narrow passages lead into underground tombs richly decorated with scenes from daily life.

2.8 Shopping

Fixed price or haggle? Cairo offers huge choice of both styles. You can shop in Cairo (and will be rewarded by a truly astonishing change in price if you bargain) for alabaster, for copper or brass, for cotton (Egypt's is among the highest grades in the world) as well as beautiful jewellery (gold and silver), leather goods and tapestries.

Khan el-Khalil Bazaars

This huge area of bazaars is spread around a maze of narrow streets. Every trade is represented from cosmetician to coppersmith, from flower seller to fortune teller. An exotic feast of Middle Eastern delight!

In the crowded alleys, motor vehicles have no chance, though donkey-carts and human porters get by. Little has changed over the centuries since trading began with building of a simple caravanserai in 1382, and then expanded during Ottoman times as a Turkish-style bazaar.

Most of the bazaars cater for local trade, from clothing and bolts of cloth to spices and furniture, caftans, dried fruit and flowers, gold bracelets. There are carpet sellers by the dozen, and enough shoe shops to serve the entire population of Cairo.

Official and unofficial guides are very happy to show you craftsmen at work. You can go from one mini-lecture to another — on carpets, perfume, inlaid work, papyrus. Through an ancient door, and you can see how antique carpets are restored and cleaned, and then hung up to dry on a rooftop.

It's a good chance to see across the rooftops of medieval Cairo. Whether you buy or not, it's fascinating!

Fixed-price shopping
In hotel shopping arcades you'll find high-quality products, but at prices geared to the potential of wealthy tourists. For more reasonable prices, go shop-gazing along the streets that radiate in six directions from Talaat Harb Square — about five minutes' walk from Tahrir Square. Most of the customers are middle-income Egyptians, and the fixed prices are plainly marked in Arabic numerals. It's worth learning the numbers, just in case the shopkeeper takes advantage. Department stores usually stay open till 8 p.m., privately-owned shops till 9 or 10 p.m.

For a high-quality shopping environment, visit the **World Trade Centre** at 1191 Corniche El Nil, near the TV Tower. The glass-roofed arcades of the shopping mall feature the finest Egyptian and international brands and products, including hand-painted furniture, silver, tableware, high-quality shirts and linens.

2.9 Eating out

Most short-time visitors to Cairo prefer to 'play safe' by eating in the leading hotels, which all have restaurants that offer a full range from elegant dining with Arabic music and floor-show to snacks at the poolside. But there's also a host of local restaurants that feature Egyptian and international food from Chinese and Indian to Lebanese and French.

All the following central hotels can offer selection of at least half a dozen restaurants and snack bars:

Cairo Marriott — It's worth going, just to gape at the Arabian Nights' setting, in what was formerly a palace. Peek inside the Aida Ballroom with its 19th-century opulence, wood-panelled walls and glittering chandeliers.
Tel: 340-8888 ext. 8266

Cairo Sheraton — The **Aladin Restaurant** specialises in superb Lebanese and Middle Eastern specialities for lunch (12.30-16.00 hrs) and dinner (20 hrs till 1 a.m.), with live entertainment in the evening. Tighten your belt all day, or you'll never make it through the full menu of mezzes, main course and dessert. Tel: 348-8600

Le Méridien Cairo — Mainly offers French and Egyptian cuisines. **Le Champollion Restaurant** features French

The Great Temple, Abu Simbel

Avenue of the Sphinxes, Luxor

Left hand page: Hypostyle Hall, Karnak

Diving in the Red Sea

A traditional Felucca

gastronomy, while their **Nubian Village** is an open-air riverside setting for Egyptian specialities and live entertainment. Tel: 362-1717

Nile Hilton — With central location on Tahrir Square, the Nile Hilton is a western oasis for lunch or a refreshment snack. Oriental snacks and burgers are served on **Abu Aly's** terrace, where you can also smoke a hubble-bubble pipe called *sheesha*. For a coffeeshop meal, try the **Ibis Café**. Tel: 767444

President Hotel — in Zamalek, **La Terrasse** features Nile views with lunchtime salad buffet, and grilled specialities in the evening. They go Chinese every Tue and Sat.
Tel: 340-0718

Ramses Hilton — Highly recommended is the dinner folklore show with belly dancing at the **Falafel Restaurant**, serving Egyptian food. There are two dazzling shows nightly, rated as the best in Egypt. Reservations are advisable. Tel: 777444 ext. 3215

Semiramis Inter-Continental — Choice of ten eating places, from sophisticated dining in **The Grill** to informal lunches and dinners with Nile views in the **Felucca Brasserie**. Tel: 355-7171 ext. 8032

Among the non-hotel restaurants, we suggest:

La Pacha floating restaurant, permanently moored on the opposite bank from the Ramses Hilton. There is a choice of seven dining rooms, and also several bars, such as Johnny's Bar and a beautiful piano bar. It's stunning!

Felfela Restaurant — downtown at 15 Kasr El Nil Street, near Talaat Harb Square. Very good value with excellent Egyptian food, in a laid-back touristy atmosphere.

Arabesque — also in Kasr El Nil Street, at no. 6. More up market than Felfela, with very good French and Lebanese cuisine.

Several other good choices are located in this area. You could pick your fancy while you're doing some evening shop-gazing.

Vegetarian restaurants

Most restaurants can concoct something for vegetarians. But as Egypt's cuisine is mainly meat-based it is advisable to check before setting off. Here's a short list:

Cairo Sheraton Hotel — La Mamma Restaurant, Italian; and La Crêperie.

Mena House Oberoi Hotel — Indian cuisine in The Moghul Room.

President Hotel — The Cellar Bar.

Semiramis Inter-Continental — Spaghetteria, and the Felucca Brasserie.

Shepheards Hotel — Asia House (Indian and Chinese).

2.10 Nightlife

With Cairo's rich daytime sightseeing potential, most short-term visitors don't have much time or energy left for vivid nightlife. Remember that shop-gazing can occupy you until 8 p.m., or even until 10 p.m. Evening meals tend to be leisurely, and comfortably fill any gap till bedtime. Most visitors want to see at least one folklore dinner show — see the dining section above for a few suggested venues. Several hotels feature elegant supper clubs with resident dance band.

Set aside one evening for **Sound and Light at the Pyramids**. Voices of the pharaohs echo through the desert, and there is powerful floodlighting and haunting music. The Sphinx does an excellent job as narrator. Dress warmly in the winter months as temperatures drop rapidly after sunset. Even in the warmer months, the desert evenings can feel chilly after the daytime heat.

Music-lovers should check what's on offer at the **Opera House**. With the main theatre and several smaller concert halls, there's usually some choice of opera, ballet, symphonic or chamber music of western type; or classical Arabic music.

Taverna life in Greek or Spanish style is non-existent. Try the Cellar Bar underneath the President Hotel in Zamalek — a highly popular venue.

Finally, a suggestion for those who like some 'real' local atmosphere. Try a late-evening visit to the Khan el-Khalil bazaar district. Towards 10 p.m. when the shops pull down their shutters, dozens of chairs are brought out to convert much of the area into an open-air café.

You can smoke a hubble-bubble pipe, and watch all Cairo life flow past. Go ready equipped with plenty of 25-piastre notes for all the disabled who live off these little gifts. A 25-piastre note can keep them in bread. There are strolling musicians, and people galore who just want to talk, without trying to steer you into shops.

Chapter Three

Luxor

3.1 Ancient Egypt & the god Amun

Luxor lies in the fertile heart of the Upper Nile valley, 420 miles south of Cairo. This 20th-century holiday resort on the river's east bank has a splendid history of almost 5,000 years.

Major growth of Luxor came in the 23rd century BC, when the Pharaoh Amenemhat I based his name on that of the city's cult deity Amun, the father of the kings. The city's power expanded still more in the 21st century, when it became capital of all Egypt.

Prosperity lasted for the 300 years of the Middle Kingdom, but declined for an Intermediate Period. Egypt was split by Hyskos invaders who used the new military technology of horses and chariots. But local kings still ruled in the south.

Upper and Lower Egypt were reunited following the expulsion of the invaders around 1567 BC. The city became the capital of the New Kingdom — the glittering power base of an empire that reached from Nubia to Palestine. Political and cultural influence stretched from the Euphrates to Libya.

In turn, the deity Amun likewise rose in importance. He took promotion and was worshipped as **Amun-Ra** — King of the Gods, a blending of sun-god Ra with Amun. Pharaohs were crowned in the deity's name. Pilgrims came to worship.

Amun-Ra's official residence was Karnak Temple, which became the focus of all the pomp of cult ceremonies. A long line of powerful rulers flourished during the 500-year golden age of the New Kingdom. Each pharaoh added to the sprawling magnificence of the temple, keeping the god happy with offerings.

Another major temple complex expanded two miles away. Today's Luxor Temple was purpose built in the 14th century BC to house Amun's vulture-headed wife Mut, the goddess of nature. Every year, Amun moved in a golden

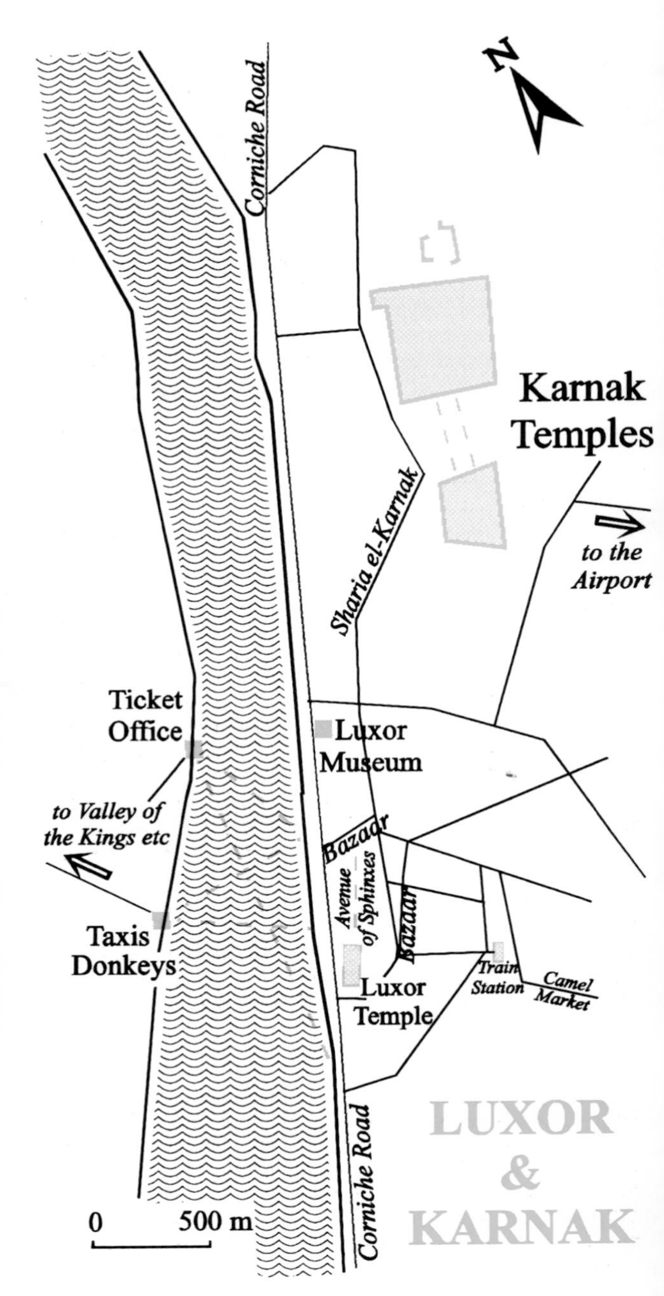
N
Corniche Road
Karnak Temples
Sharia el-Karnak
to the Airport
Ticket Office
Luxor Museum
to Valley of the Kings etc
Bazaar
Avenue of Sphinxes
Bazaar
Taxis Donkeys
Luxor Temple
Train Station
Camel Market
LUXOR & KARNAK
Corniche Road
0 500 m

river barge to Luxor Temple for an annual 17-day honeymoon, with parallel human ceremony and all the carnival atmosphere of the Opet Festival.

During its history, the city had various names. Originally it was called Weset, a word that symbolized rule and authority. When Greeks visited the city, they linked the name of its sacred places with their own city of Thebes. Homer's *Iliad* described Thebes as 'the hundred-gated city', and the poet enthused over the grandeur of its walls and temples. At its peak, ancient Thebes had an estimated population of one million.

Other writers followed suit in calling the city Thebes. The Greeks equated the city's deity with their own Zeus, the supreme god. For that reason Alexander the Great renovated the inscriptions on the walls of Luxor Temple, and had himself portrayed as a Pharaoh, kneeling in the presence of Amun-Ra.

In the 7th century AD, the Arabs were equally impressed by the architectural scale and called it the city of El Uqsor — the City of Palaces. With time, this was converted to Luxor in other languages.

Luxor today rates as Egypt's most beautiful resort, with dry air and clear skies. In a week or two there's time to make leisured exploration of the world's greatest record of ancient civilisation. The east bank temples for the living were balanced by the mortuary temples and tombs of the western hills.

Paintings, carvings and sculptures open up an incredibly rich world of gods, pharaohs, noblemen and ordinary folk, with their varied life-styles depicted in every detail.

But Luxor offers much more than culture-vulture sightseeing. Most visitors make time for relaxation — sun-bathing beside the hotel pool, sailing on the river, taking a traditional cruise, or strolling through the bazaars.

Just outside Luxor there's all the colourful life of rural Egypt, where many scenes haven't fundamentally changed over the past 5,000 years. There are palm groves, gardens with exotic flowers, and friendly people everywhere. Luxor has every ingredient for a memorable holiday.

3.2 Arrival in Luxor — orientation

On the air approach to Luxor, you look down to the blue Nile and its network of irrigation canals. The rich green of cultivated land cuts off sharply at the edge of the desert hills. There is no gradual merging of green and yellow. Either the land is irrigated, and is teeming with life; or, if not, there is only gaunt yellow desert, an awesome moonscape.

The living and the dead

Luxor's green east bank is the City of the Living. The desert west bank — apart from a green fringe of sugarcane — is the City of the Dead. East bank has the great temples of Luxor and Karnak. West bank has the incredible tombs and mortuary temples: Valleys of the Kings and Queens; The Tombs of the Nobles; the Colossi of Memnon and the Ramesseum.

On the town side, orientation is easy. All the big hotels are located along the riverbank Corniche — from Sheraton and the Old and New Winter Palace, just south of Luxor Temple, and past Etap Hotel and Luxor Museum to Karnak and thence to the Hilton.

The Luxor Hilton has a peaceful riverside location a mile beyond Karnak Temple, with a free on-the-hour mini-bus shuttle to the gates of Hotel Egotel, in the town centre. That's the tourist heart of Luxor, with bazaars hugging tightly to streets around the Luxor Temple site.

3.3 Local transport

Distances in Luxor are quite small, but you'll often be glad of a short ride. Stroll along the Nile bank, and you'll be flooded with offers of local transport: taxis, horse-carriages and feluccas. Ask your rep for guidance on what to pay. The going rate can vary according to season, but mostly will depend on whether you start a haggling session knowing what's reasonable.

Horse-drawn carriages — There's an olde-worlde charm about riding in a carriage. Even if you're not very expert at the haggling game, the price for a ride is far less than for a similar jaunt in any European resort. Whatever you agree, the cabbie will still pitch for baksheesh on top.

Ferries — Public ferries shuttle back and forth to the west bank, where fleets of tour coaches, taxis and donkeys await. For a standard circuit of the scattered west bank sites, reckon an overall total of 20 miles. So take your pick of transport.

Feluccas — The felucca boatmen who make you run the gauntlet of their sales patter are plainly descended from a long line of double-glazing salesmen. They pursue you with discount after discount, never taking 'no' for an answer until you reach the territory of another felucca tout, and there's yet another verbal hurdle to pass.

However, at some time during a stay in Luxor, don't miss going for a sail. When agreeing your final price, be totally sure you are talking Egyptian or English pounds. A favourite trip is two or three miles upriver to Banana Island. Go ashore, see bananas and citrus growing, and buy some to eat. Try it one afternoon, timed for a return at sunset. Idyllic!

Horse-riding — A recommended stable called Adel-Brenda with Arabian horses is located across the river. Take the local ferry in front of Luxor Temple. On arrival, follow the asphalt road for some 400 yards to the Mobil filling station. The stables are away to the left. No hard hats are available, so bring your own from Britain.

Bicycles — If you feel mildly energetic, it's easy to rent a bike by the hour or the day. Traffic around town is fairly relaxed, and you can soon reach the countryside. On the west bank, the hills make cycling a sweaty option, and you'll need to take quantities of water.

Balloon safari — It's a pricey experience, but a cooler way of sightseeing than by bicycle or donkey. Depending on wind direction, you float over Luxor's greatest attractions, taking a sun-god's view of the human life and temples below. A free breakfast is included. In peak summer months, weather conditions may prevent operation.

3.4 Basic Luxor — East Bank

At whichever hotel you're staying, the principal sites of Luxor are all within extremely easy reach — Luxor and Karnak Temples, and the Museum.

Decide whether you prefer to tackle the temples yourself, or to take a guided tour. Do-it-yourself, you'll save money — though you still have to budget LE 10 for each temple, and some transport and baksheesh. But unless you are a dedicated student of ancient Egypt, there are dozens of details which you'll miss on your own — even if you pick them out with a heavyweight guidebook. An accredited tour guide can bring all those details to life, giving you a crash course on the workings of ancient Egypt. Here's a brief outline of what's in store.

Luxor Temple

This magnificent and well-preserved temple lies in the centre of Luxor, facing the banks of the Nile. On the site of a former temple, it was founded by Amenophis III (1405-1367 B.C.) as a private palace for the god Amun. On the walls, Amenophis traced his own descent from the deity.

During the Nile flood, Amun's effigy made the short journey up-river from Karnak, to enjoy an anniversary honeymoon with his wife, Mut. The ceremonies helped ensure that the Sacred River would continue to bear riches to the land. The fertility festival marked a good time for everyone, with general debauchery.

Major additions were made by later rulers including Tutankhamun, Ramses II and Alexander the Great.

Admission to the site is through a ticket gate on the Corniche side of the complex. Entrance to the temple itself is through an enormous gateway marked by a huge statue of Ramses II (1290-1224 B.C.). Two seated statues of Ramses II flank the pylon. Beside them are two other statues of Ramses II, standing. Even the non-expert can guess who built this part of the temple.

Also in front were formerly two large granite obelisks. One was removed to the Place de La Concorde in Paris, but its twin still stands in the original location.

The route leads into a courtyard built by Ramses II, surrounded by columns which were roofed to form arcades. In the north-eastern part stands the Mosque of Al Haggag. It was built long before the Temple was excavated, and is still in use.

Next comes a Colonnade of 14 pillars, with crowns in the shape of papyrus flowers. On the walls, Tutankhamun inscribed scenes of the festivities of Amun.

Among the great highlights is the Amenophis III Courtyard, with majestic columns carved to represent bundles of papyrus. The adjoining Hypostyle Hall has a ceiling supported by 32 columns in papyrus design. The walls depict religious rites.

VIP territory

Finally one reaches the inner sanctums, which formerly were accessible only by priests and VIP's. A centre chamber was used as a church in early Christian times. Another contains the story of the birth of Amenophis III, with evidence of his descent from the god Amun. A third chamber shows Alexander the Great, dressed like a pharaoh, making offerings to the god Amun. Finally we reach the four-columned Holiest of Holies: the Sanctuary of the Sacred Statue.

Today there is some threat to the site because of the rising water table — a problem brought by the Aswan High Dam. The water attacks the foundations, and much work is needed at Luxor to counter this problem.

A one and a half mile long avenue leads to the temple of Karnak. On both sides are statues of the Sphinx, with a ram's head and the body of a lion.

Temples of Karnak
Dating from the 20th century BC, this complex of temples was the official residence of Amun, king of all the gods, and a centre of administration.

For over 1500 years the Pharaohs constantly enlarged its area, building mighty temples and statues, sacred halls and courtyards, until the site became the largest place of worship known to man. Its original name was 'Ipetisut', meaning 'the most perfect of places'. Here, major religious ceremonies were held, while the Pharaohs sought inspiration from Amun-Ra, from whom they claimed direct descent. Since the Arab conquest, the site became known as 'al-Karnak': the Fort.

In the main courtyard, major festivities were celebrated. Individual temples were dedicated to Amun-Ra, his wife (Mut), and their son (Khonsu), the moon deity. The three of them — Amun, Mut and Khonsu — formed the Theban Triad.

A visit to Karnak begins at the quay of the sacred boats, where markings indicate the level of the Nile flood. An avenue of ram-headed sphinxes leads to the temple entrance — the First Pylon. Every visitor pauses to photograph the line-up of rams on each side — symbols of fertility and growth. Beneath the rams' heads are carved small sculptures of Ramses II.

Through the First Pylon, a massive entrance corridor leads into a courtyard with a temple each side. To the left is a 3-chapel temple, built by Seti II to house the sacred boats of the Theban Trinity.

To the right is a Temple for the Theban Trinity, built by Ramses III. This building is the world's first example of basilica design.

Next comes the Great Hall of Pillars — also known as the Great Hypostyle Hall — equipped with 134 columns. A dozen of them have capitals in Papyrus form. This Great Hall was built in the days of Seti I and Ramses II.

The Hall of the Obelisks houses two obelisks: one for Tuthmosis I and the other for his daughter Queen Hatshepsut. This latter obelisk is 100 feet high — the tallest still remaining in Egypt — with an estimated weight of 320 tons. A somewhat taller one was removed from Karnak by Emperor Constantine in 357 AD and was finally re-erected in Rome during the 16th century, where it was given the name of the Lateran Obelisk. Incidentally, Rome altogether has 48 Egyptian obelisks scattered around the city.

Every stage brings you to a still older part of the complex. The Hall of Ceremonies was built by Tuthmosis III, on the site of an old temple from the days of the Middle Kingdom (21st Century BC). Wall decorations illustrate

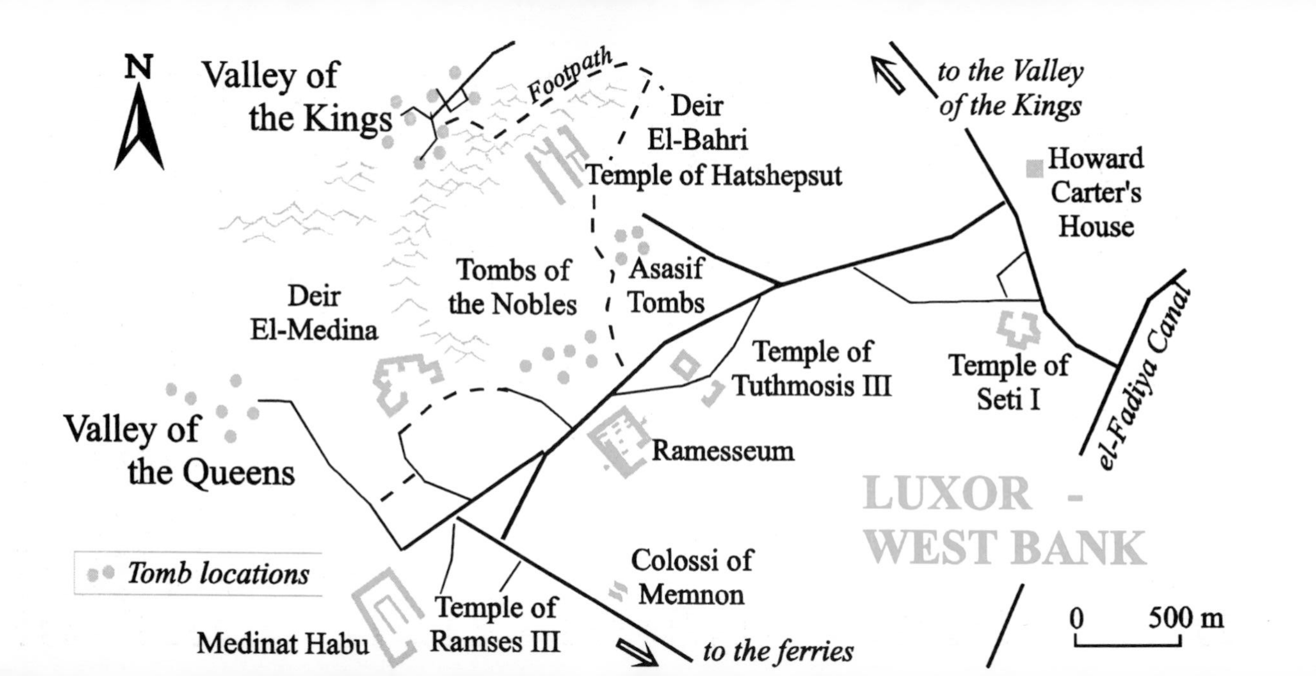

N
Valley of the Kings
Footpath
Deir El-Bahri
Temple of Hatshepsut
to the Valley of the Kings
Howard Carter's House
Deir El-Medina
Tombs of the Nobles
Asasif Tombs
Temple of Tuthmosis III
Temple of Seti I
el-Fadiya Canal
Valley of the Queens
Ramesseum
LUXOR - WEST BANK
Tomb locations
Colossi of Memnon
Temple of Ramses III
Medinat Habu
to the ferries
0 500 m

plants, animals and birds collected by the Pharaoh during a tour of Asia.

The Sacred Lake, lying east of the Hall of Ceremonies, was used by the priests for ritual purification. It is now overlooked by seating accommodation for the final part of the night-time Sound and Light show. Near the refreshment kiosk is a huge statue of a Scarab Beetle from the days of Amenophis III, who built The Temple of Luxor.

Luxor Museum

This small but well-displayed museum is open daily for five hours every evening — from 4 p.m. during winter, or from 5 p.m. in summer. The times change during Ramadan. It faces the river promenade, exactly halfway between the Temples of Luxor and Karnak.

3.5 West Bank

A visit to Luxor's West Bank is a major highlight of any trip to Egypt. That's where so many tombs of kings, queens, noblemen and priests are located. Colours of tomb paintings are incredibly well preserved despite their age of well over 3,000 years. That is explained by the bone-dry storage conditions of the rock-cut desert graves. Guides explain why the tombs were built and how they were equipped and furnished to meet their tenants' plans for afterlife in the underworld, and ultimate resurrection.

The fantastic detail of the paintings covers every aspect of life in ancient Egypt: religious beliefs, and the mythology of the gods; the triumphs of war and peace; the lives of pharaohs, or farmers, musicians, fishermen, soldiers, traders, acrobats, scribes, bureaucrats or tax collectors. Every aspect of life and events is closely recorded, to make Ancient Egypt far better documented than any other pre-Christian society.

While paintings show most of these details, still more information is written in the hieroglyphs — from the names of kings to a precise Book of the Dead which is like a guidebook to the underworld.

When the capital was located at Memphis near present-day Cairo, pyramids were in fashion for royal burial. But the tomb-building professionals of Thebes followed a much less labour-intensive burial style which avoided the logistics of hauling huge chunks of stone around.

The chosen burial sites in the desert hills west of the Nile were beyond reach of the annual flood waters. There was symbolism about the orientation. The sun rose in the east, over the city and temples of the living. It set over the tombs and mortuary temples of the dead.

Tombs and temples for each pharaoh were deliberately kept separate. There was relatively easy access to temples built in memory of the major rulers, sited just outside the edge of river flood and cultivation. But the actual tombs were set further back, honeycombed into desert-valley hillsides — separate valleys for kings, queens and nobles.

Tomb diggers and decorators had a job for life, handing down their secrets from father to son. The assignment was to make access difficult enough to defeat grave-robbers. As soon as one pharaoh was buried, and his tomb fully equipped with food, furniture and knick-knacks for the afterlife, work would immediately start on a tomb for his successor.

That explains why Tutankhamun's tomb — though it yielded such a fabulous horde of treasure — was relatively modest. He died young, having ruled only nine years. So the workforce hadn't made much progress with construction of his burial vault. Completion was done in a rush. It was ironic that this quick job of tomb-building was missed by all the later grave-robbers until Egyptologist Howard Carter found the tomb in 1922. That was after he had spent six seasons in dedicated shifting of many thousands of tons of sand and rubble that concealed the entrance.

Centuries earlier, every other pharaoh's tomb had been cracked open and looted. Priceless art-works were just melted down for the metal.

Just like on the East Bank, visitors have the choice of buying a guided tour or making up their own circuit. Two or three people can share a taxi, for a half-day tour of the main sites.

However, a cab-driver just takes you to each entrance, leaving you to make your own interpretation of the paintings and to understand what the hieroglyphs are saying. An accredited guide can open your eyes to far more than even the most detailed guidebook with coloured pictures.

What to see

There's an embarrassment of riches which can keep an enthusiast happy for weeks. But here's a typical itinerary for a lengthy morning sightseeing tour, just to give the flavour:

- Two major temples — of Queen Hatshepsut and of Ramses II (the Ramesseum);
- Valley of the Queens — tombs of Prince Amun Herkhepshep and of Queen Titi;
- Tomb of Ramose;
- Valley of the Kings — two or three tombs, possibly from a short-list of Ramses III, Ramses IX, Seti I, Amenophis II and of Tutankhamun (if open);
- The two Colossi of Memnon.

The order of the listing has no significance, but a selection of these sites would be included in average sightseeing packages. Tour guides shuffle the sequence, to avoid having too many groups queuing simultaneously at each site. Even so, some traffic jams at favourite tombs is unavoidable.

The Ramesseum

This was the mortuary temple of Ramses II, who made his mark as a strong ruler during his 67-year reign. He was a big-time builder, responsible for Abu Simbel, the massive entrance to Luxor Temple, and additions to numerous other sites. His mortuary temple acted like an obituary notice for posterity, paying special tribute to his war record. He took obvious pride in having defeated the Hittites at Kadesh virtually single-handed. Decorations show highlights of the battle. There are horses, chariots, archers — some triumphant, others dead or dying.

All over Egypt, this larger-than-life character has left behind gigantic statues of himself, including a selection at Luxor Temple. The largest of all — 1,000 tons of pink granite — stood here in the Ramesseum. Regrettably it was destroyed by Persian invaders, who conquered and ruled Egypt twice. The Persians hated the pharaohs. So, when they conquered the country, they vandalised these masterpieces everywhere.

In the Ramesseum the pharaoh's giant statue was knocked down, and today lies scattered in pieces — his head, an elbow, a knee-cap — all scattered. Ramses II originally stood 63 feet high, 25 feet across the shoulders, and had ears that measured 3½ feet. The poet Shelley wrote about the pharaoh's downfall in his work 'Ozymandias', scoffing at Ramses' dream of immortality. But it must be acknowledged that the life and deeds of Ramses II are probably better known than for any other pre-Christian king — a form of immortality.

The Colossi of Memnon

These two immense statues, 66 feet high, formed part of a monumental avenue that led to the funerary temple of Amenophis III (14th century BC) which has long since crumbled away. The temple site is now occupied by acacia trees. Amenophis was the pharaoh who founded the Luxor Temple.

Each statue was carved from a single block of sandstone. The left-hand statue was reputed to give out musical sounds every morning — possibly vibrations caused when the rock was warmed by the rising sun. None of the Greek and other historians who visited the site could give any explanation of this phenomenon, which gave birth to a suitable legend.

The Greeks named the statues after Memnon, the legendary hero killed by Achilles during the Trojan War. Each morning he called his mother Eos, the Dawn goddess; and she bewailed him, shedding tears that were the dewdrops.

The statue was damaged by earthquake in 27 AD, but was then restored by Roman emperor Septimus Severus, who visited Egypt in 199 AD. He hoped that renovation would re-activate the statue's musical abilities. But ever since then the monument has remained mute.

Queen Hatshepsut Temple

This dramatic three-level temple is cut into the base of a limestone cliff. As you walk towards the temple, you can see part of the necropolis dating from about 1600 BC. To the right of Hatshepsut Temple are Tombs of the Nobles. Each opening is one tomb.

The Valley of the Kings can be reached by a steep path, up and over the mountain — a hot 45-minute hike, or easier by road in an air-conditioned coach. Valley of the Queens is to the left. Orientation is confusing, as the roads into the valleys must take roundabout routes.

The Temple of Queen Hatshepsut was built 3500 years ago. Its three-tier design made good use of the cliff's natural slope. The upper level was later converted by Coptic monks into what was called the 'northern monastery' — Deir el-Bahri in Arabic.

This protected part of the site from dilapidation, though the monks vandalised some of the decoration. The temple remained visible through the centuries, but the lowest terrace was completely covered by rubble that crumbled down the mountainside.

Hatshepsut was the queen pharaoh of the 18th Dynasty, ruling from 1473-1458 BC. She came to power when she married her half brother, Thutmosis II. When he died, there was a power struggle between Hatshepsut and her stepson-cum-nephew (son of her brother-husband by another wife). At first they shared power, but later Hatshepsut forced her stepson to abdicate. When Hatshepsut died, her stepson Thutmosis III came back to power, and took revenge by hacking out her name from the temple, and obliterating her face. Such was family life among the pharaohs — almost as complicated as marital arrangements among the gods and goddesses!

However, Queen Hatshepsut has come down in history as a shining light of the 18th Dynasty. In minute detail, bas-reliefs depict a trading expedition deep south into Africa, to the mysterious land of Punt, which probably was

Somalia. The aim was to collect incense, hennah, myrrh and ivory. The mission travelled by a fleet of galleys, via the Red Sea and down the east coast of Africa. The houses, trees, birds and animals of Somalia are depicted. The Red Sea is shown with many types of fish, which can readily be identified — turtle, sea-bass, swordfish, butterflyfish, squid and lobster.

The local top brass of Somalia is shown raising their hands in welcome of the trading mission. The Queen herself suffered from elephantiasis, and is portrayed weighing heavily on an unfortunate donkey.

Valley of the Queens

Around 75 tombs have been identified, relating to queens of the 19th and 20th dynasties, and some of their near relatives. But only four of the tombs are open to visitors.

The **Tomb of Prince Amun Herkhepshep** is the most interesting. He was the adored son of Ramses III, but died aged nine. Paintings show the prince being groomed by his father for his future role as Pharaoh, with personal introduction to the gods. The final introduction was to the jackal-headed Anubis, god of the dead, who leads the boy down to the burial chamber. A somewhat gruesome relic is displayed — a mummified fetus, reputedly aborted by the Prince's mother out of grief at Amun's death.

Tombs of the Nobles

Several hundred tombs of the nobility have been located, and at least a hundred have something more to offer than just a hole in the ground. Inscriptions and paintings give a detailed picture of the lives of the aristocracy and their families.

The **Tomb of Ramose** is of special historic interest, covering a transition period when the priesthood of Karnak briefly lost power to the monotheistic worship of Aten. Ramose was a state official during the reigns of Amenhotep II and Akhenaten — the latter king being responsible for the heretical idea of worshipping one god only. A striking scene depicts Akhenaten and his wife Nefertiti, standing on a balcony, with nobles pledging their loyalty.

Valley of the Kings

If you arrive here at midday, you'll appreciate the full power of the Egyptian sun to dessicate any living growth. It's a parched rocky area with steep cliff sides and no vegetation.

Once the kings were mummified, and placed deep within their burial chamber, there was no way in which any moisture could penetrate. Their bodies would be preserved for immortality. Likewise the story of their lives and deeds in carvings, paintings and hieroglyphics would last across thousands of years, so that their historic memory became immortal.

Altogether, of the 62 tombs which have been excavated, only a limited number are accessible to visitors. An entry ticket gives admission to any three tombs that may be open, but Tutankhamun's tomb requires a separate ticket. Even so, that tomb is often closed, partly because of the sheer weight of tourist numbers.

The Tomb of Ramses IX

From the entrance gate, the first tomb on the left was tenanted by Ramses IX. A lengthy corridor leads to an antechamber, a hall with pillars and finally the burial chamber. A ceiling painting depicts the sky-goddess Nut with a good supply of stars.

The Tomb of Seti I

Rated as the best preserved of the tombs, it extends over 100 yards down into the hillside. It is famous for its reliefs, depicting the worship of the sun, and also scenes that show the sun's journey at night in the lower world. If the tomb is closed for restoration, you can see the King's sarcophagus in London's Sir John Soane Museum.

Tomb of Tutankhamun

As mentioned above, the tomb of Tutankhamun is very modest in comparison with that of kings who lived much longer. But everyone wants to visit the tomb which yielded such great treasures. Walls are painted with vividly coloured scenes of religious rites. Discovered in 1922, all the fabulous contents of the tomb were moved to the Egyptian Museum. Only the Middle Sarcophagus remains with the King's mummy inside.

Tomb of Ramses III

Taking 45 years to build, the large burial chamber itself is not accessible to the public. But there is great interest in the long descending passages with ten side chambers, richly decorated with etched hieroglyphics and figures of the king and his servants.

Tomb of Amenophis II

This tomb goes very deep, with a deep pit designed to deter grave-robbers. However, thieves still managed to loot everything, but left a dozen mummies intact, to be discovered by French archaeologists in 1898. The wall decorations have kept their colour.

3.6 Take a trip

Luxor is an excellent base for side-trips to the other main highlights of Upper Egypt.

Upstream to Aswan

If you have made arrangements in advance, the best option is a two-centre deal, preferably with cruising in between the two cities — staying a night or two in Aswan to explore in detail.

Otherwise, consider one-day Aswan by air. It's more expensive than surface travel, but is the best way of seeing the highlights of Aswan — High Dam, Philae Temple, a felucca ride, and possibly lunch at the Old Cataract Hotel, part setting for Agatha Christie's *Death on the Nile*.

By road in a convoy, it's a 4-hour journey each way — even longer if a stop is made at a temple en route. That makes up a very long, hard day.

Downstream towards Cairo

There are chances to see the Temples of Denderah and Abydos, either by coach tour or — better — by one-day or two-day Nile cruise boat. In recent times, however, Abydos and sites north in Middle Egypt have been 'off limits' for security reasons. Hopefully that situation may change by the time you travel.

3.7 Shopping

As a lasting memento of what you've seen of Ancient Egypt, it's worth buying one or more coffee-table books, filled with superb colour photos. There are some excellent productions on the market.

Many small shops in Luxor sell brass, alabaster, jewellery etc, preceded by the usual mini-battle of haggling before a deal is made. Typical purchases could include camels for any children on your present-list, maybe a bottle opener, packs of playing cards, a silver pendant of Queen Nefertiti, tea cloths and a scarab.

Some vendors may try to persuade you to buy a 'genuine' antique, with authenticity backed by a plausible story. If the artefact is really genuine, export would be illegal.

On the West Bank, guides often stop to show you how alabaster products are made by craftsmen who sit cross-legged at their work, using tools that are replicas of those used in ancient Egypt. Suchlike tools were originally made of a special bronze metal that was hard as iron. But most of the alabaster on sale today is machine-made.

3.8 Eating out

In and around Luxor there is good choice of either hotel-based or local restaurants that cater for all pockets and tastes.

Mövenpick Hotel Tel: 374855

This Swiss-run hotel has probably the best buffet in town and excellent service. Themed food nights cover everything from American food evenings to the most elegant Italian evenings. The Mövenpick is set in beautiful grounds on Crocodile Island. You can also cross by boat during the day and sample their excellent Ice Cream Sundaes.

Old Winter Palace Tel: 371189

In this ornate old palace, now a 5-star hotel, they offer afternoon tea in the Victoria Lounge on the terrace overlooking the Nile. In the 1886 Restaurant they serve Nouvelle Cuisine in a formal setting. Likewise formal dress is required, and a table should be reserved in advance.

Egotel Hotel Tel: 373321

Outdoors in the grounds is an excellent oriental restaurant, featuring Egyptian food in an oriental setting, with seating on cushions. On some evenings there is traditional entertainment.

Isis Hotel Tel: 373366

Has a variety of restaurants including Chinese, offering good value and good food.

Sheraton Hotel Tel: 374955

La Mamma's Italian Restaurant has top notch service and the best Italian Pizza in town.

Jems Restaurant

Located near the Isis Hotel, it serves a choice of Egyptian and International food in a beautiful setting, where the wall decor will keep you entertained throughout your meal.

Class Tel: 386327

This restaurant near the Isis Hotel offers the best range of starters and the most friendly service in town.

Peace Restaurant

In a beautiful riverside setting in the village of Karnak, this restaurant serves a wide range of fish dishes.

Flamboyant Restaurant Tel: 380944

For something a little different, this à la carte restaurant at the Etap Hotel offers excellent service and a good menu.

Maxim's

Near the Sheraton, Maxim's offers a variety of international food.

3.9 Nightlife

Temples of Karnak, Sound and Light Show
Utterly mesmerising! Stroll by night among the floodlit temples of Karnak to the accompaniment of dramatic music and commentary. The 90-minute spectacular takes you on a conducted tour through the labyrinth of passages and corridors to which only priests and the pharaohs had access. Finally you take your seat beside the Sacred Lake, where the epic story, music and light display continues for the latter half the show. Don't miss it!

Normally there are two shows each evening: 8 p.m. and 10 p.m. in summer, but earlier in winter and during Ramadan — with a rotation of Arabic, English, French and German through the week. At the second performance, it's cooler and less crowded.

The dramatised script describes the great kings and queens, gods and goddesses. You cannot miss the story of Ramses II, the great warrior pharaoh who did so much temple-building, and who normally thought in terms of statues a hundred feet high. As part of the royal life-style, Ramses II — who reigned for 67 years — was married to three queens. After the third queen he married four of his own daughters. He fathered 92 boys and 106 girls.

A voice declaims that "It was here in Karnak that He who is called Amun sat upon a hillock and thought the world into being during the floods of the month of July."

A little later, Amun himself speaks: "My right eye is the day. My left eye is the night. And the waters of the Nile spurt from my sandals."

It's a great story: two thousand years of ancient Egyptian history, brought to life in its authentic setting.

Other evening entertainment
In Luxor most evening entertainment is based in the hotels, and also on some cruise boats.

Sheraton Bar & Disco — Listen to live singers and music in the bar and dance the night away in the Sheraton Hotel Disco.

Lotus Boat — Tibas Star — Disco boat floating on the Nile, attracting locals as well as tourists.

Hilton Casino — A great place to try your luck at Black Jack, Roulette etc.

Kings Head Bar — An English style bar in the centre of Luxor, where you can meet ex-pats.

Discos are also located in the Etap Hotel and the Egotel.

Chapter Four

Aswan

4.1 The frontier town

For the best introduction to Aswan, treat yourself to tea on The Terrace at the Old Cataract Hotel — also known as Hotel Pullman Cataract. Since the hotel opened in 1902, The Terrace has offered a god's-eye view of the historic highlights of Egypt's most southerly city.

Just up-river was the awesome First Cataract, where the foaming waters in ancient times marked a boundary between Upper Egypt and Nubia. The ancients reasoned that here dwelt the cataract god Khnum in his cavern, from where he arranged the annual flood that gave life to Egypt.

Your teatime Terrace looks directly over the southern end of Elephantine Island, where grey-black rocks still look like a herd of Jumbos' taking a bath.

A cluster of temple ruins are a reminder of when Aswan was the gateway to Africa. On the island stood the original frontier and fortress town of Yebu — a great trading centre where ivory and skins were brought down the Nile from Nubia. Temples were dedicated to Khnum, and to the local Nile deities called Hapy and Satet.

Egypt became the world's first bureaucracy. You can see the bulging outline of the Nilometer, where revenue officials of the Ancient Egyptian civil service measured the height of the July floods and calculated what should be the yield in taxes, paid in kind. According to the Greek historian, Herodotus: "Egypt is the gift of the Nile." The pharaohs took their share, to finance the building of temples and pyramids that assured them eternal life.

Just above the Nilometer — marked by a splendid sycamore tree — is the red-roofed villa which now operates as a modest Aswan Museum. The villa was built for the British architect of Aswan's Old Dam, completed 1902, which pioneered the present-day taming of the Nile.

Several mud-brick Nubian villages encroach at the edges of the original sprawling temple site. The Nubian life-style

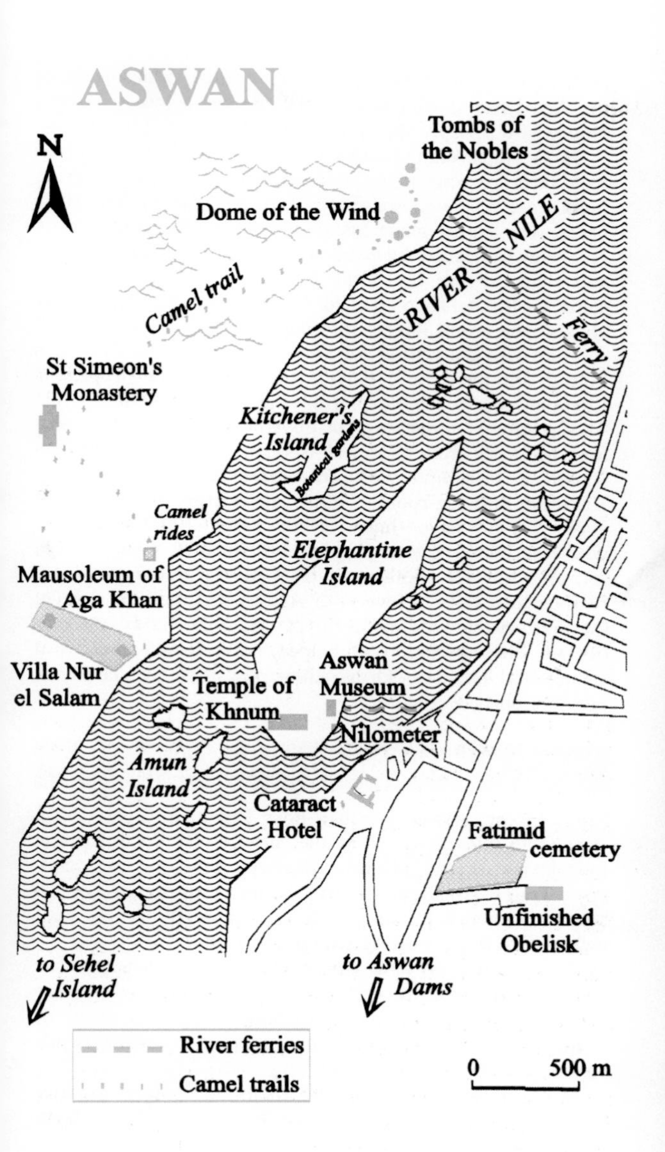
ASWAN
N
Tombs of the Nobles
Dome of the Wind
RIVER NILE
Camel trail
Ferry
St Simeon's Monastery
Kitchener's Island
Botanical gardens
Camel rides
Elephantine Island
Mausoleum of Aga Khan
Villa Nur el Salam
Temple of Khnum
Aswan Museum
Nilometer
Amun Island
Cataract Hotel
Fatimid cemetery
Unfinished Obelisk
to Sehel Island
to Aswan Dams
River ferries
Camel trails
0
500 m

still flourishes, despite relocation necessitated by the High Dam's flooding of their homelands. Black goats and grey donkeys meander along the pathways. Directly across the river, on the West Bank, the 20th-century Mausoleum of the Aga Khan is silhouetted on the tawny-coloured hilltop. Notice how sharply the landscape changes into pure desert.

In the intervening waters of the Nile, graceful feluccas waft their passengers on blissful circuits of the riverside highlights; or there are motor launches and sedate cruise boats. The entire scene makes up one of the great classic Nile views, framed by palm trees that offer rich greenery and shade. From the hotel Terrace you can walk down steps to the feluccas parked below, waiting for wealthy clients who won't haggle too much.

Here was the setting for sequences of Agatha Christie's "Death on the Nile". Savour the atmosphere of prewar Egyptian tourism by exploring the hotel's public rooms. The interior is something out of Arabian Nights, with two-tone Moorish arches, carved wooden screens, and Nubian waiters in 19th-century Ottoman dress. The lift is a mobile Victorian drawing-room, with ornate mirrors and a leisured pace. Try to have dinner at the Club 1902 restaurant, where so many famous people have dined. It's like a stage set, all ready for another Agatha Christie mystery.

Everyone falls in love with Aswan. Go there to unravel the mystery of what made Egypt: the Nile floods, the cult of Isis, the quarries that helped build temples, colossal statues and obelisks. Or go there just to relax, laid-back beside a shaded pool.

4.2 Getting around Aswan

From Luxor, Aswan is a half-hour EgyptAir flight with a speedy 14-mile drive from the airport. By road, reckon four hours for the 143-mile journey, travelling in a convoy. Trains take four or five hours from Luxor, or 15 hours by overnight sleeper from Cairo. By cruise boat reckon five days, visiting temples en route.

Aswan itself presents no problems of orientation. The Corniche follows the east bank of the Nile, with other main streets running parallel. Make a special point of wandering along Sharia al-Souk and its immediate side streets, for the bazaar quarter.

Most of the holiday hotels, shops and travel agencies are located along a one-mile stretch of the Corniche from Ferial Gardens to the Tourist Office.

When you tire of strolling along the promenade, just surrender to the sales pitch of cabbies, horse-carriage drivers and felucca boatmen.

There is no equivalent road on the West Bank, but well-used camel trails lead from a boat landing-stage to the Aga Khan's Mausoleum, Saint Simeon's Monastery and the Tombs of the Nobles. The Tombs can also be reached by ferry from opposite the Tourist Office.

Another useful public ferry goes from the Ferial Gardens (at the south end of the Corniche) to Elephantine Island, conveniently dropping you by the gate to Aswan Museum and the Nilometer. Of the principal sites, the Unfinished Obelisk is within walking distance of Ferial Gardens. Bike hire is feasible for reaching the High Dam and the boat jetty to Philae. Otherwise take the easy way of a guided package tour, or haggle with the cabbies.

4.3 Basic Aswan

The Unfinished Obelisk

Obelisks were sacred symbols to the Sun God. The four gently tapering sides represented rays of the sun that widened as they reached earth. Obelisks were normally erected in pairs at the entrance of temples, with suitable inscriptions. A visit to a work-site just outside Aswan helps one understand how such enormous monoliths were cut and transported. Aswan's quarries were a prime source for the rose-red granite used in construction of temples, obelisks and colossi. Abandoned work on the Unfinished Obelisk sheds light on the working methods of ancient masons.

The recumbent Obelisk is 140 feet long, with a 13-ft square base. If completed, it would have weighed 1,168 tons, and would probably have been the world's largest. However, during cutting, the obelisk was found to be fractured, and work was abandoned. It had been detached from the bedrock on all except its lower face.

Its history is unknown, though it probably dates from around the 15th century BC. The obelisk carries no inscriptions, as that work would normally have been done after the monument had been finally cut out.

Two sides of the obelisk were detached by cutting channels which were filled with wooden wedges and soaked with water. The resulting expansion then helped separate the stone from its mother rock. One still marvels how the ancients envisaged removing such a weight of stone — except that it was downhill all the way! Barge transport is well documented in relief sculptures elsewhere.

Obelisks have been popular souvenirs of Egypt for the past 2,000 years. The Roman emperors collected 13 of them for erection in Rome. Other fine specimens are located in Florence, New York, Istanbul, Paris and London.

The Aswan Dams

The ancient Egyptians divided the year into three seasons of four months each: Flood, Winter and Summer. The inundation started in June with great regularity. The Nile rose above its banks and flooded the countryside. When the waters receded in October, farmers re-established their field boundaries, planted seed in the richly fertile deposit of silt, and harvested their crops in due time.

But the volume of Nile waters was unpredictable. A good flood one year could be followed by drought; fat years followed by lean. From earliest times, efforts were made to regulate the Nile by storage ponds and irrigation canals, with marginal success.

In the 20th century, however, the Nile has been tamed and harnessed. The first stage came in 1902, with completion of the British-built Aswan Dam above the First Cataract, just south of the city. It heralded the beginning of modern irrigation in Egypt. The present-day road from the airport on the West Bank crosses the crest of the Old Dam, built of granite from local quarries used by ancient temple-builders. For many years this rated among the world's largest dams, a showpiece of civil engineering. In 1912 it was raised from its original height of 130 feet to 147 feet; and then further raised to 155 feet in 1934.

After the 1952 revolution which ousted King Farouk, the new-broom government commissioned a feasibility study for building a High Dam at Aswan, 4 miles south of the existing dam. German consultants drew up a mammoth plan to store the whole of the Nile flood-water, feeding it to downstream fields month by month, while boosting Egypt's electricity capacity.

A political decision by Britain and USA in 1956 to cancel promised loans led directly to Nasser's nationalization of the Suez Canal to fund the High Dam project. Later the Soviet Union came through with an aid package. Soviet engineers with a labour force of 30,000 Egyptians worked round the clock from 1961 till 1971 to complete the job. That Egyptian-Soviet cooperation is marked at the High Dam by a pink granite monument that represents a stylized lotus, dominating the skyline.

A visit to this spectacular site should not be missed. The crest of the dam — two miles long, and 364 feet high — is wide enough for a three-lane highway, lined with decorative trees, grass and flower-beds watered by sprinkler systems. There's a lay-by for spectators' cars and tour coaches. Photography is permissible at this authorised viewpoint, but use of video camera or zoom lens is forbidden. Guards are also twitchy about visitors who stop for pictures elsewhere on the dam.

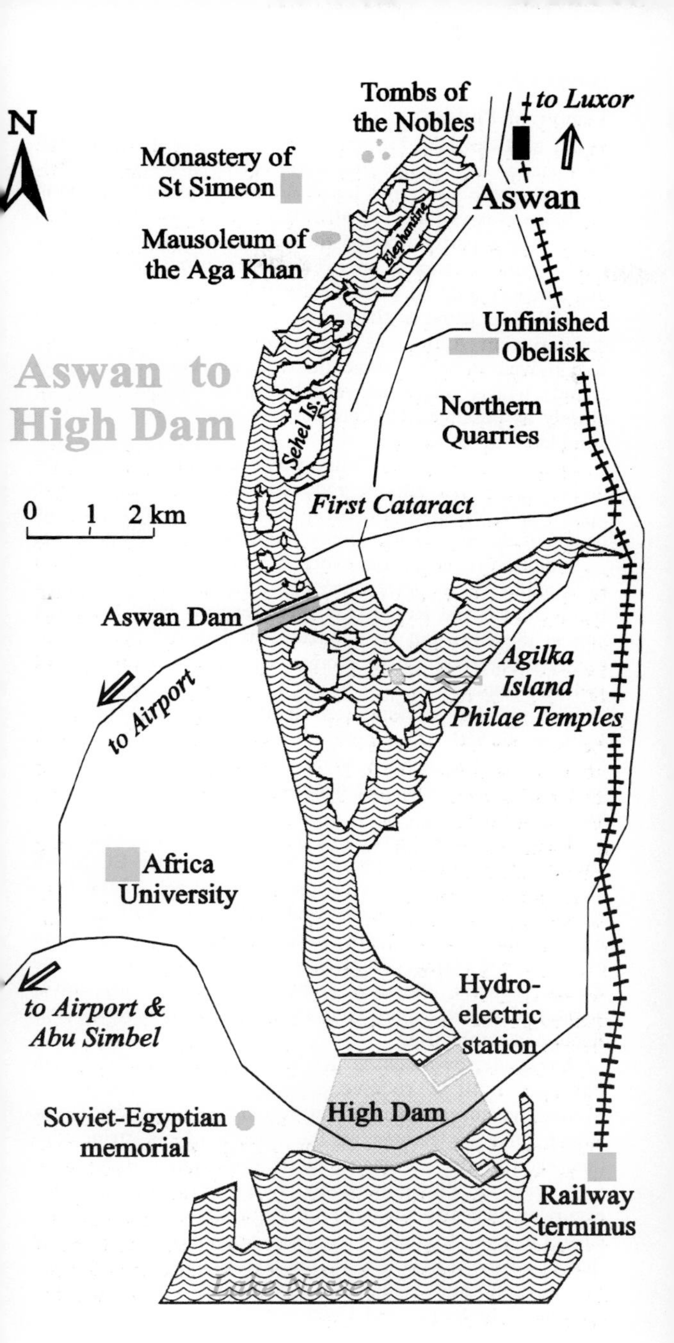
Tombs of the Nobles
to Luxor
N
Monastery of St Simeon
Aswan
Mausoleum of the Aga Khan
Elephantine
Unfinished Obelisk
Aswan to High Dam
Sehel Is.
Northern Quarries
0 1 2 km
First Cataract
Aswan Dam
Agilka Island
Philae Temples
to Airport
Africa University
Hydro-electric station
to Airport & Abu Simbel
High Dam
Soviet-Egyptian memorial
Railway terminus
Lake Nasser

Temple of Philae

In the artificial lake formed between the Old and the High Dam stands the Temple of Philae, on the island of Agilkia.

The temple's original home on the neighbouring island of Philae was endangered after building of the first Aswan Dam, which partly flooded the island every year. But the High Dam threatened an even more serious problem — that Philae would be permanently submerged.

UNESCO came to the rescue. In a joint operation with the Egyptian Antiquities Organization, the entire temple was moved stone by stone onto the neighbouring Agilkia island, which was even reshaped to resemble Philae as closely as possible. This project took eight years, and was completed in 1980.

From earliest times, Philae was a great religious centre dedicated to the cult of goddess Isis. The location was significant, close to the first cataract: regarded as the origin of the annual life-giving flooding of the Nile.

Tradition required that every Egyptian should come here to worship Isis at least once in a lifetime. Even pilgrims from Greece and Rome paid their respects until relatively late in the Christian era. Indeed, the Isis cult was Christianity's big rival in the Roman Empire between the 3rd and 5th centuries.

The worship of Isis was finally banned by Emperor Justinian in 550 AD. Coptic Christians then took over the Philae Temple, defaced some of the carvings, chiselled crosses on the walls, and dedicated the church conversion to St. Stephen.

The sanctuaries were built mainly during the Ptolemaic and Roman periods — roughly from 4th century BC to 4th century AD. There are well preserved scenes of the Pharaohs worshipping the gods, and of Ptolemy XIII sacrificing prisoners of war to the divine husband and wife team of Horus and Hathor. In Hathor's own Temple, east of the Temple of Isis, the cow goddess of beauty, joy, love, dance and music is portrayed enjoying the playing of harp, flutes and tambourine.

Alongside, overlooking the Nile, is the beautiful Trajan Pavilion, built to receive processions of sacred boats. Modern visitors arrive further round the island by motor launch, and are greeted by the screech of one-string violins, each fiddler-salesman playing something different.

A visit to Philae normally forms part of a half-day excursion that also includes the High Dam and the Unfinished Obelisk. A guide is virtually essential, to get the full flavour of the stories told by the hieroglyphs and carvings. For a night-time view, the details show up even more vividly in the Sound and Light performance.

Elephantine Island

A short ferry ride from the landing stage just north of the Old Cataract Hotel brings you to Elephantine Island, which rates as the oldest inhabited area of Aswan. As a frontier post guarding routes to the south, the original town of Yebu sprawled at the southern end of the island, where varied remains have been excavated.

Crossing by public ferry or private felucca, disembark just by the **Aswan Museum**. A modest collection of Aswan and Nubian relics — mainly from Greco-Roman times — is on display in what formerly was a villa owned last century by Sir William Willcocks, the architect of the first Aswan Dam. Take a stroll around his garden, scented with flowers and spice plants.

Museum exhibits include pre-dynastic pottery and a range from Pharaonic times — necklaces, scarabs, surgeons' instruments, ivory hair-pins, statuettes, amulets, pottery and tools. There are varied mummies of priests and priests' wives, with golden decoration. A golden mummy of the sacred ram is fitted with a mask representing the god Khnum.

The entrance fee also covers admission to the Nilometer and to the ancient ruins beyond.

Only a few yards from the ticket kiosk, beneath a sycamore tree is the rock-carved shaft of the **Nilometer**, which measured the height of the Nile in flood. This measuring device enabled priest-economists to predict the extent of inundations downstream — July until October — and thus forecast a fat or lean year's harvest. Depending on the expected crop yield, taxation rates could be set to meet the required levels of public expenditure.

The original Nilometer from Pharaonic times was rebuilt during the Roman era. Re-discovered in 1822, it was again restored in 1870 — hence the inscriptions in French and Arabic — and remained in use until recently. There are inscriptions in Greek and Arabic, besides the cartouches of Pharaohs Thutmose III and Amenophis III — proving that the Nilometer must have been used at least from the period of the 18th Dynasty, 3500 years ago.

Heights were measured in cubits — the length from the human elbow to the tip of the middle finger. A text at Edfu Temple notes that when the river rose 24 cubits (about 12 metres) there was enough water to supply the needs of the whole country. The Greek writer Plutarch said the Nile once rose here to a height of 28 cubits — over 14 metres or 46 feet.

Relics of ancient temples are scattered around some 300 acres of the ancient town of Yebu, which meant both Ivory and Elephant in ancient Egyptian. Grey-black granite rocks in the river look like elephants enjoying a dip. Chief deity of the region was ram's-headed Khnum. He looked after the Nile cataracts, and also created human beings on a potter's wheel.

The **Temple of Khnum** was rebuilt in the 30th Dynasty (4th century BC). Alexander II — the short-lived son of Alexander the Great — came here as King of Egypt around 80 BC to pay his respects, and added a splendid entrance gate which depicts him dressed like an Egyptian Pharaoh presenting offerings to the gods.

North of this temple lies the temple of Ptolemy VII (2nd century B.C.). Other temples are dedicated to Seti I and Ramses II.

A well on the island is credited with mankind's first calculation of the earth's circumference. Pythagoras and Aristotle had already argued that the earth was spherical. Then, around 250 BC, at noontime on the longest day of summer an observant character noticed that the sun's rays descended perpendicularly into the well, without casting a shadow.

He passed on this information to Eratosthenes — a Greek geographer who was chief librarian at Alexandria, due north. He deduced that the sun, Aswan and the centre of the globe were in a direct line.

At Alexandria, Eratosthenes waited till the next summer solstice, and then measured the noontime angle of the sun's rays at one-fiftieth of a full circle — about 7½ degrees. Knowing the approximate distance from Aswan to Alexandria, simple geometry enabled him to calculate the circumference of the earth to within 15% accuracy.

In the palm groves between the Museum and the perimeter of the lofty Aswan Oberoi Hotel are three **Nubian villages**. If invited to explore the alleyways, you'll find a fascinating lifestyle. Some house facades are decorated in the brighter colours of the spectrum. These are traditional communities, unwilling to be part of the tourist circuit. So be tactful about photography, and don't wear ultra-brief shorts!

Several other islands add interest to a felucca cruise. **Amun Island** is the site of a Club Med development.

Kitchener's Island

A classic felucca cruise around the river islands is the most blissful form of Aswan sightseeing. Depending on the deal with the boatman, you could take a short trip to watch the sunset, or a longer ride to visit Kitchener's Island and the Mausoleum of Aga Khan.

Kitchener's Island is now officially known as Aswan Botanic Island. The 16-acre Botanical Gardens are possibly the finest in all Africa. The oval-shaped island is divided into 27 main sections, each devoted to a different area or family of equatorial plant life.

Its origins date from 1898, when the island came under the wing of the Ministry of Irrigation. In 1928, the site was turned into an experimental station for plants of equatorial origin. In the perpetual warm sunshine of Luxor, this came cheaper than making the trials under glass in Cairo.

The Botanic Island features a wide collection of good timber trees; also of oil-bearing trees such as the coconut palm; a selection of fruit-bearing trees from cashew nut to papaya, citrus and guava; spice crops such as ginger and cinnamon; all kinds of plants that could have a medical use; and those that yield fibre products.

Among the plants and trees are ebony, banana, pomegranate, bread tree, sausage tree, sycamore, poinsettias, ipomea, morning glory, moonflower, periwinkle, acacias, many species of palm, orange tree, hibiscus, jasmine, bougainvillaea and rubber plant. Royal Palms form a superb avenue with their slender light-grey trunks that soar ramrod-straight to their green crown.

The island is also a great place for bird-spotting. Typically, in May when fledgelings are at their most demanding, there is colossal noise from trees where dozens of egret families are nesting. The young flutter up and down the branches, hollering for lunch, which finally is rammed down their throat by an overworked parent. With a telephoto lens, you can easily capture some of the scenes which the layman normally sees only on TV.

The gardens include some sad-looking caged monkeys, and a more cheerful and noisier enclosure of pea fowl from India.

Mausoleum of Aga Khan

Highly visible on the west bank is the white-domed Mausoleum of Aga Khan III, who died in 1957, aged 80. Famed for his great wealth, the Aga Khan was also the Imam — religious leader — of the Ismaili sect of Shi'ite Muslims. He originally came to Aswan to fix his rheumatism, but liked the location so much that he built a hillside villa and returned every winter. His hilltop mausoleum is an exquisite example of Fatimid architecture.

Disembarking at the landing stage, you run the gauntlet of souvenir salesmen who awaken to life at the arrival of every boat. Good views reward those who climb the hot flight of steps, or who ride up by camel or donkey. Modestly dressed visitors can enter the monument and view the Carrara marble tomb, decorated with a single red rose in a silver vase.

4.4 Other sights

After you have explored basic Aswan, a few oddments still remain if you have the time. Varied travel-agency tours include the sites in a felucca package with time ashore.

Across on the West Bank is **St. Simeon's Monastery**. Access is by boat to the landing-stage close to the Aga Khan Mausoleum, and then aboard camels or donkeys — unless you prefer to walk — to the site at the end of a desert valley.

Dating from 6th century AD, when the worship of Isis was banned, St. Simeon's is Egypt's best-preserved Coptic monastery. Housing 300 monks, the fortress-like monastery was enlarged in the 10th century. It was used as a missionary base into Nubia, where the monks converted the people to Christianity. When Christian Nubians then used the monastery as a launch-pad for raids on Islamic Egypt, the anti-Crusader warrior Saladin destroyed the buildings in 1173. The basilica is still sometimes used for church services. Frescoes of Christ and the Apostles can be seen on the walls, but have long since been defaced.

Tombs of the Nobles

If you have already seen Luxor's Valley of the Kings, then Aswan's Tombs of the Nobles are really for the dedicated. These rock-tombs honeycomb the western hills, opposite the northern tip of Aswan. A public ferry crosses the river from a landing-stage near the Tourist Office. Then walk uphill. Dating from 23rd century BC onwards, inscriptions and paintings depict the nobles who controlled the trade with Nubia, mainly during the Old and Middle Kingdoms. As defenders of Egypt's southern border, they also led expeditions into Nubia.

4.5 Shopping

The street market of Aswan is a delight. Just head for Sharia al-Souk and you'll find the entire bazaar quarter, very central, three blocks east of the Isis Hotel. Apart from a few shops and stalls which are pitching for tourist trade, most of the shoppers are locals in quest of spices, fruit, vegetables or pigeons.

The spice stalls are richly coloured, with prices that are far lower than anything you'd pay back home. Black-robed women walk along with plastic shopping baskets on their heads. During market hours, the streets are a pedestrian precinct, with donkey-carts counting as pedestrians.

The people are noticeably different from the Egyptians further north. A spin-off from the High Dam was that thousands of Nubians relocated around Aswan. They have handsome faces like mahogany wood-carvings. In this classic trading post, you can feel Aswan's role as the gateway to Africa. With discreet use of camera, you can capture that rich ethnic diversity.

There's fascination in watching bakers, cobblers and vegetable salesmen at work, and seeing the shop displays of cloth, shoes, pots and pans. It's all quite safe, except for bicycles which have no warning bells.

4.6 Nightlife

Nobody goes to Aswan for the nightlife. An evening stroll along the Corniche is about the wildest it gets. Several leading hotels feature dinner and floor show, while Aswan's Cultural Centre offers Nubian folk performances.

Philae Sound and Light

Even if you have already visited the Temple of Philae by day, don't miss the Sound and Light performance. The show is presented as a theatrical play, rather than being filled with historic dates and figures. It's a drama of gods and goddesses, in one of Egypt's most romantic locations.

The first half is spent walking through the temple precincts. In the second half, you are seated. The entire show lasts about 50 minutes.

By coloured floodlights, the temple bas-reliefs stand out even more sharply than by sunlight. Hieroglyphs look like newly-printed symbols on a page. The music, commentary and dialogue all add to this melodrama under the stars.

The basic story is pure soap opera. Isis marries her brother Osiris, who is tricked into a coffin and drowned in the Nile by her wicked brother, Seth. Isis finds the coffin, and brings it home. But the body is removed by Seth, who cuts it into 14 pieces which are scattered around Egypt. Isis finds the dismembered parts, builds temples and sews Osiris back together. The restored Osiris makes love to Isis, who then gives birth to their son Horus. Nicknamed The Avenger, Horus kills wicked uncle Seth and lives happy ever after.

There are two performances nightly, with a rotating schedule of languages. Travel agents offer a hassle-free evening package, to include hotel pick-up, taxi or motor-coach transport, entrance, and motor-launch to the island. On a do-it-yourself basis, be prepared for keen haggling with cab-drivers and boatmen.

Chapter Five

Lake Nasser

5.1 Saving the past

If you are standing on the High Dam at Aswan, look south for a fine panorama along Lake Nasser, which backs up for 310 miles, on average 6 miles wide. It's the world's second largest artificial lake, after Lake Kariba that borders Zambia and Zimbabwe. A thriving fishing industry is well established.

The northern parapet of the dam overlooks the hydro-electric installations that have doubled the country's previous output. Six main tunnels drive a dozen underground turbines which have spurred development of metal and artificial fertilizer industries. Villages throughout Egypt are now electrified, and electric pumps replace donkey or ox power to irrigate farmers' fields. Controlled irrigation has expanded crop areas by 30%.

However, the creation of Lake Nasser has also caused problems. Large areas of Nubia were flooded, and 100,000 inhabitants had to be relocated. Intensive studies were made by archaeologists, photographers and historians to record the Nubian homeland before it was submerged. International action saved Abu Simbel and several other temples, but much more has been drowned. Silt which formerly spread fertility along the Nile valley is now building up on Lake Nasser's bed.

From Aswan there are possibilities of road access to some of the salvaged temples, or even to visit Abu Simbel by air. But more recently cruise-boats have been operating on the Lake, to offer the more relaxing experience of enjoying the slow unfolding of desert vistas.

The Temple of Kalabsha

Closest to Aswan, on a promontory on the west bank of Lake Nasser, is the relocated Temple of Kalabsha. This is one of Nubia's largest sandstone temples, ranking as the finest building in Nubia after Abu Simbel.

From Aswan the temple can be reached by a one-hour drive, possibly followed by a boat-ride when the waters of Lake Nasser are high enough to make Kalabsha an island. A splendid causeway leads up from the water's edge to the main gateway. Open 6-17 hrs daily.

The temple was moved in 1970 from its original site some 30 miles further south, as part of a UNESCO rescue funded by the West German government.

Dating from the reign of the Roman Emperor Octavius Augustus (30 BC — 14 AD), the temple was originally built on the site of an earlier sanctuary founded by Amenophis II.

The temple was dedicated to the Nubian fertility god Mandulis (whose local name was Marul). Carvings depict ancient Egyptian deities, including Isis, Osiris and Horus. Later the temple was used as a Christian church, complete with Coptic inscriptions and a carving of St George. There are excellent rooftop views over Lake Nasser.

Kiosk of Kertassi

On a small hill southwest of the Kalabsha Temple are the remains of the Kiosk of Kertassi, which likewise has been relocated from its original site 25 miles south of Aswan. Built during the time of the Ptolemies in honour of the goddess Isis, two of the six salvaged columns are crowned with the cow symbol of Hathor, the goddess of beauty, love, joy, dance and music. The hilltop offers good views of Lake Nasser.

Beit el-Wali Temple

Northwest of Kalabsha is the rock-hewn Temple of Beit el-Wali, which means 'House of the Saint'. It is one of the five Nubian temples built by Ramses II (1279-1213 BC), and was relocated with US financial aid. It comprises an open courtyard, a hypostyle hall and a kiosk, with multi-coloured texts and inscriptions.

Battlefield scenes in vividly coloured bas-reliefs show Ramses victorious over Cushites, Libyans and Syrians. Erected at the beginning of his very long reign, the temple was purpose built to commemorate Ramses' conquest of the Nubians, and shows him receiving appropriate tributes of ivory, gold and animals. In turn, Ramses is shown making offerings to Horus and Isis.

The temple was used as a church during Coptic times, and was then decorated also with Christian themes.

Wadi El Seboua

The temple at Wadi El Seboua — meaning 'Valley of the Lioness' — takes its name from the sphinxes which form an impressive approach to the monumental gateway. It was built during the reign of Ramses II and dedicated to the Sun-God Re-Harakhte, Amun-Re and to Ramses himself, who was worshipped as a god. This is another of a group of temples relocated by UNESCO.

El Dakka

The Roman-era Dakka Temple dates from the Meroitic and Ptolemaic Period and is dedicated to Thot, the god of the moon, divine wisdom, and the inventor of writing,
Lord of time and the sciences. The Greeks equated him with Hermes.

The temples at El Dakka and Meharaka were documented in 1905-7 by the first Egyptian Expedition of the Oriental Institute, led by James Henry Breasted, who copied and translated inscriptions from monuments that were formerly inaccessible or in a state of decay.

Meharaka

A Greco-Roman temple, small but exquisite.

Amada

Dedicated to the pharoahs Amun-Re and Re-Harakhte, the rock-cut temple of Amada was built during the reigns of Thutmose III (1479-1426 BC) and his son Amunhotep II (1426-1400 BC) of the XVII Dynasty (1567-1320 BC). Thutmose III was crowned king at age 10, learned military skills in his 'teens and even commanded a military campaign in Nubia at an early age.

In later campaigns he consolidated Egypt's power in Nubia and set the Nubian tribesmen to work in gold mines which funded his building of temples and other public monuments.

The temple at Amada, decorated with brightly painted reliefs, is the oldest on Lake Nasser. In Christian times the temple was used as a church, and the reliefs were covered with whitewash, which had the effect of preserving the original colouring.

Close by is the temple of **Ed Deir**, and the rock-cut **Tomb of Penut**, the viceroy of Nubia from the time of Ramses VI (reigned 1145-1137 BC).

Kasr Ibrim

Located on the east bank of Lake Nasser, and still in its original site very close to the Sudanese border, the hilltop fortress of Kasr Ibrim briefly marked the most southerly point of Roman occupation.

Around 22 BC a Roman army led by the prefect Petronius captured several towns of the Meroitic kingdom, gained the submission of the ruling queen, and established a garrison at Kasr Ibrim, which the Romans called Primis.

But this occupation of Lower Nubia soon ended, with the Romans pulling back to around 50 miles south of Aswan. The fortress was converted into a mosque in the 14th century. When Egypt was absorbed into the Ottoman Empire in 1517, Sultan Selim the Grim placed a garrison of Bosnian soldiers here, to control Nubia. The fortress was occupied in 1812 by the Mamelukes and in the same year Ibrahim Pasha recaptured and destroyed it.

The summit of Kasr Ibrim is today strewn with remains from the Nubian, Roman-era and Ottoman times.

5.2 Abu Simbel

The greatest and most famous of the Nubian temples is located only 30 miles from the border with Sudan, where Lake Nasser becomes Lake Nuba. An early evening arrival at Abu Simbel by cruise-boat is made even more memorable by floodlighting, with the dramatic prospect next morning of seeing sunrise on the monuments.

Certainly, if you're not visiting Cairo and the Pyramids, Egypt's most fabulous highlight must be the temples of Abu Simbel, 170 miles south of Aswan — a four-hour drive across the desert. EgyptAir operates regular flights daily to the site, made world famous by the international rescue operation that saved Abu Simbel from being drowned in Lake Nasser.

The engineering achievement was incredible. Carved into the rock face, the Great Temple was the grandest of the monuments built by the hyperactive Pharaoh Ramses II who ruled from 1304-1237 BC. The facade measures 110 feet high and 130 feet wide, guarded by four enthroned statues of Ramses himself, somewhat larger than life at 66 feet high.

For over 3000 years the temples have remained virtually intact, except for disfiguring of statues which were originally covered in gold. The Great Temple pays homage to the sun god, Ra, while a smaller temple is dedicated to the cow-goddess Hathor and to Queen Nefertari, a Nubian, the favourite wife of Ramses II. Her temple is fronted by four standing statues of Ramses, but only 33 feet tall; and two of Nefertari.

In a dramatic race against the rising waters of Lake Nasser, Swedish engineers carved the structures into over a thousand blocks of sandstone which were lifted for precision re-assembly 215 feet higher up the cliff face. Look at the monument today, and you cannot see where or how the 30-ton blocks were joined together.

Water marks still show from inundations at the original location. A protective concrete dome is rated as the world's largest.

The four statues of Ramses II are deeply impressive in the sunshine, with sand martins circling around. In the great hypostyle hall, eight pillars all represent Ramses, 33 feet in height, protected by the vulture god Osiris. Carvings and paintings depict Ramses in a chariot, defeating a Hittite army virtually single-handed. Modesty was not part of the Ramses character profile.

A second, smaller hall has four square pillars with reliefs of Ramses and Nefertari making offerings to the gods. Then comes the sanctuary with its four statues of Ra-Horakhti, Ptah, Amun and Ramses II.

In its dedication to the sun-god, the Temple faces east. Twice a year — on the anniversaries of Ramses' birthday and of his coronation — the rising sun reaches directly into the innermost chamber to light up the faces of Ramses and two of the gods: but not Ptah, who is the god of darkness.

For visitors who travel each way by road, it makes a long day for the round trip from Aswan. But the journey across the desert offers the excitement of seeing mirages, camel caravans and Bedouin camps. A day to remember! The more leisured cruise-boat travellers normally journey one way by the Lake, the other by road.

Chapter Six

Nile cruising

6.1 Classic touring in hotels afloat

Leisure is the keynote. Maybe many mornings you'll be up and away early on a temple sightseeing before the sun gets too hot for comfort. But then you return to your floating hotel for lunch, siesta and sun-bathe. The pattern is soon established: cruise and relax; awake to five o'clock tea and cake; 8 p.m. dinner; and then some kind of shipboard entertainment, or time ashore for a Sound and Light show. If you just want a quiet hand of cards or Scrabble, a selection of games is available.

Cruise-boats are fitted to the standards of 3-star or 4-star hotels, with deck-top swimming pools, sun deck with sun beds, and canopied terrace with tables and chairs.

Accommodation is in outside cabins, with full air-conditioning, large picture windows (though windows on the lower level do not open), shower and w.c. en suite, telephone (not ship to shore) and radio.

Public areas are tastefully decorated. A spacious dining room and deck-level lounge/bar are air conditioned. Friendly staff are on hand round the clock. All meals are included, and you sign for drinks. Your bar bill at the end of the voyage can be paid in cash, travellers cheques or plastic. Money exchange is possible only when a bank clerk comes aboard once or twice during your cruise.

Guides remain on board throughout the cruise, and are always glad to answer questions. Always remember to check the cruise notice board for details of the day-by-day programme.

Which cruise itinerary?

Today's cruiseboats are mostly based on Luxor, to offer great flexibility of 2-night, 4-night and 7-night options that concentrate on the highlights of Upper Egypt.

A typical pattern is to start from Luxor, cruise downstream to visit the important temple of Denderah; return for the Luxor sites; then continue to Aswan. That means 7 nights for the full package or 4 nights for Luxor-Aswan.

These cruise packages can then be dove-tailed with hotel stays ashore in Luxor or Aswan.

Watch Egypt float by

Gliding along, you can enjoy a blissful panorama of riverside life. It's an unending stretch of greenery, dominated by the waving heads of palm trees. In their shelter are tiny fields of vegetables, clover for animal feed, rice and maize. Elsewhere are plantations of bananas and other fruits, or sugar cane. Domestic animals graze peacefully.

Little villages of mud-brick houses are the same colour as the river banks — all formed from the same centuries'-old deposits of Nile silt. Through binoculars you can see hundreds of little vignettes of village life — men and boys trotting along on donkeys, farmers labouring in the fields, women pounding clothes at the river bank, children returning from school.

Cattle are brought down to the river's edge for a paddle. An occasional camel lopes along, or a donkey cart. There is rich birdlife.

Birds of Egypt

A slow-moving cruise boat makes a perfect platform for bird-watching. Don't forget to take binoculars. Below are some of the birds that you may spot, depending on the season and whether the birds are resident or migrant. During the migration months of autumn and spring, the green valley of the Nile, rich in food, makes a natural route between Europe and Central Africa. Some birds stay for the winter.

White stork — Common migrant, especially south of Qena. Often soars in large flocks; bill and legs red; lives off insects and small animals.

Osprey — Migrant bird and winter visitor. Always found near water, eats fish.

Kestrel — Resident breeding bird and winter visitor. Often found near villages. Eats rodents and insects.

Cattle egret — Abundant resident breeding bird, nesting in colonies in trees near habitation. Buffy feathers on crown, back and breast during breeding season. Feeds on insects in fields.

Turtle dove — Common migrant bird found in large gardens and farmland. Long tail with a lack of spots on lower neck.

Laughing dove — Abundant resident breeding bird in towns and villages. Black spots on lower neck and short tail.

6.2 Sites between Luxor and Aswan

The 140-mile cruise between Luxor and Aswan features three major sites — Esna, Edfu and Kom Ombo. The volume of river traffic can mean delays at Edfu lock, which may entail re-scheduling of some trips.

Sometimes Esna lock is closed for maintenance. This likewise entails revision of itineraries, with some sectors of the tour operated by escorted coach or mini-bus.

Temple of Esna

Dedicated to the god Khnum, who created men and animals by moulding them from Nile clay. The temple originated during the period of the New Kingdom (1570-1100 BC) and lies deep below present-day street level. It has not been fully excavated.

The existing remains date from Ptolemaic-Roman times. The hypostyle hall has pictures and texts telling of the Roman emperors who came to Egypt and offered sacrifices to local deities.

Temple of Edfu

This is Egypt's best-preserved temple, dedicated to Horus the god of the sun and plants. His falcon image is represented in two majestic Ptolemaic statues in black granite, guarding the temple entrance. A 'young' temple, it was completed by Cleopatra's father in the 1st century B.C.

The present-day town of Edfu is a market centre with sugar mills and a long-established pottery industry. It is located about 65 miles south of Luxor, on the west bank of the Nile.

Temple of Kom Ombo

Twenty miles from Aswan, the temple of Kom Ombo stands on a sweeping bend of the river bank where sacred crocodiles once basked in the sun. This temple is unusual in being dedicated to two gods: Sobek and Haroeris, each with his own entrance and sanctuary. Sobek was the crocodile god of Nile fertility. Haroeris, also known as Horus the Great, was the solar god of war.

Most of the reliefs date from the time of Ptolemy XII. Among the details is a set of medical instruments.

Spot the collection of mummified crocodiles in the Chapel of Hathor.

Irrigated land in this area is mainly devoted to sugar cane. Many of the local people are Nubians, resettled from their former villages, inundated when the High Dam created Lake Nasser.

Temple of Denderah

Cruises north of Luxor stop at Qena to visit the very well preserved Denderah complex of temples. The main temple is dedicated to Hathor, mother of the gods and wife of Horus. As befits her maternal status, Hathor was represented as a beautiful woman, a fertile cow or sometimes as a mixture of both. Columns are decorated with the head of the goddess.

The worship of Hathor at Denderah was started by King Cheops around 2600 BC, close to the river and about 40 miles north of Luxor. But today's Greco-Roman temple was built between 116 BC and 34 AD. The temple was inaugurated by Ptolemy III with numerous additions by subsequent rulers. It houses a famous painting of Queen Cleopatra, and Caesarion, her son by Julius Caesar.

The temple is famed for a ceiling carving depicting the signs of the zodiac; and also for a representation of the sky goddess, stretched out to hold up the sky.

Despite its proximity to the river, Denderah lies on the edge of the desert. There is access to the roof for a far-ranging view. The annual Nile flood waters were kept out by an immense mud-brick wall, much of which still remains.

Sites further north, towards Cairo, have in recent years been 'off limits' for security reasons. For this reason, cruise-boats have not operated past Denderah, though there is a possibility of limited resumption.

Chapter Seven

Sinai and the Red Sea

7.1 Coral reefs and desert

Sinai Peninsula and the Red Sea have come relatively late to the tourism feast. When the Israelis occupied the entire Sinai Peninsula in 1967, some tourist facilities were built along the Sharm el Sheikh coastline. After the Camp David agreements between Israel and Egypt in 1979, most of the territory was returned to Egypt by 1982. Since then, new international-grade hotel complexes have extended themselves along favoured beaches with powder-fine sand of egg-timer quality.

In similar style, new resorts along the Red Sea coast are attracting international visitors — either those who are totally dedicated to the under-water life, or others who want to split their time between the beaches and the classic sites of the Nile Valley.

7.2 Sharm el Sheikh

This resort at the southern tip of the Sinai Peninsula is a location for all ages — from couples who just want to relax under beach umbrellas, to school-holiday family groups. None of the other winter-warmth destinations within a 4-hour flight of Europe, such as the Canaries or North Africa, can be so confident of non-stop sunshine.

The resort hotels are completely self-contained, offering a full range of watersports, dive facilities, choice of restaurants, informal bars and small shops.

Likewise, evening entertainments are in-house, revolving especially around the bar-discos. In the Hilton's Fayrouz Village, the Oriental restaurant features a top-grade floor show, full of vitality — a spinoff from Cairo's highly-rated show at the Ramses Hilton. Performances change several times each week, so you could go at least twice without repetition.

Although Sharm el Sheikh seems remote from the Nile experience, two-centre holidays are feasible. EgyptAir operates several flights weekly to connect with Cairo or Luxor. The capital is also accessible on a six-hour drive by bus or coach; and there are ferries across the Red Sea to Hurghada.

There is far more to the resort than the gorgeous sandy beaches. Scuba divers regard the area as the Mecca of the sub-aqua world, thanks to perfect conditions along the emerald-green coast. They rate the Gulf of Aqaba and the Red Sea as paradise, with incredibly rich and varied flora and fauna, including over 1,000 species of fish and coral.

The coral reefs of the Aqaba Gulf are judged to be much better than those of the Caribbean or East Africa. To explore this underwater world is an unforgettable experience.

Most of the Gulf of Aqaba seaboard is now completely protected as the Ras Mohammed National Park. The first protection law was passed in 1983. Since 1989, when the Ras Mohammed Protected Area was classified a National Park, the boundaries of the Marine Park have been greatly extended and also for miles inland.

Over one half of the Gulf of Aqaba coastline is now protected, and the rest is managed. Following the latest extension around St. Catherine's Monastery, 10% of the Sinai Peninsula's land area is National Park, with an EC-financed British manager in charge.

What started as a Marine Park has also had great efffect on birdlife, both resident and migratory. There has been a dramatic increase in bird numbers since the Park was created, linked with a complete hunting ban in the Sinai.

Osprey breeding groups are expanding in number, and resident wader species are also increasing. Migrating birds of importance include the white stork and the black stork, both of which were formerly endangered. Large numbers of raptors such as falcon, buzzards and kites follow these migrations.

Biblical connection

Much fascination comes from seeing first-hand the beauty of the region which has played such a big part in Biblical history — Moses, the Burning Bush, the Ten Commandments, wandering in the wilderness.

The visitor can experience some of that Biblical history by visiting St. Catherine's Monastery — the peninsula's foremost sightseeing highlight. In between the saw-toothed granite mountains are valleys of finely-sifted sand, with only an occasional Bedouin village or encampment where one can stop for tea.

7.3 The Sinai in history

Despite its desert nature, Sinai has always played a vital part in history as a Middle Eastern land bridge between the continents of Asia, Africa and Europe. The name Sinai may be derived from a religious cult devoted to the moon-goddess Sin.

According to the ancient Egyptians, the goddess Isis wandered across Sinai during her search for her murdered husband and brother, Osiris. The land was mined for gold, copper and turquoise. Indeed, Sinai was the world's first major source of turquoise, with hard-rock mining dating from 3400 BC.

Besides its Biblical role as the route of the Israelite Exodus under Moses, Sinai has been better documented as a battlefield on which Egyptians fought one enemy after another from the time of Ahmos I (1567 B.C.) when he drove out the Hyksos armies across Sinai, till the more recent wars with modern-day Israel.

In between those dates, Sinai has been overrun by Assyrians, Hittites and Babylonians; retaken by Egyptians; and then subdued by Persians and Greeks, Romans, Arabs and Ottoman Turks.

In 1479 B.C., Thothmes III led his Egyptian armies across Sinai in the earliest recorded Egyptian campaign designed to achieve greater unity in the region and punish invaders. Details of that campaign are recorded on the Wall of Records in Luxor's Karnak Temple.

In 333 B.C. Alexander the Great crossed Sinai with his armies to clear out the Persians and instal the Ptolemaic Dynasty. In 48 B.C. near Port Said, the armies of Queen Cleopatra met those of her brother Ptolemy in a civil-war battle.

In Biblical history, the Holy Family fled across Sinai into Egypt. At every spot where the Holy Family is reputed to have rested, a church now stands. The last major invasion armies across Sinai were those of Islam under Amr Ibn El-As in 639-40 AD.

St. Catherine's Monastery

The prime sightseeing attraction of the Sinai Peninsula is the Orthodox monastery of St. Catherine's, which is among the oldest of the Christian world. Located 220 kms from Sharm el Sheikh, it's a full day trip — long trousers needed, not beachwear, otherwise no admittance!

In the heart of a rose-red rock landscape, overlooked by Mount Sinai high above sea level, St. Catherine's is an independent complex which has for centuries been a place of pilgrimage.

Monastic life began in this location during the 3rd century AD, when Greek Orthodox monks established a hermitage around the legendary site of the Burning Bush where God spoke to Moses. The monks wanted to be in total isolation from the outside world, dedicated to a life of prayer. Around 327 AD, St. Helena — the mother of Constantine the Great — funded the Chapel of the Burning Bush.

From time to time the monks were exposed to attack and plunder by Bedouin tribesmen. As an additional hazard, Sinai was on a traditional invasion route. In 527 AD Emperor Justinian gave the community monastery status, and ordered the building of a basilica. Fortress walls and a resident garrison of 200 guards ensured safe refuge to monks and pilgrims.

Today, the original granite walls are still in good shape — 3 metres thick, between 8 and 25 metres high, and up to 300 metres long on each of the four sides. Even though the monks have dwindled to around 15, the complex still remains a working monastery. Suitably dressed visitors are admitted inside the fortress walls, and can visit the basilica, the treasury and a large collection of icons. A highlight of the basilica is a famous mosaic, similar to its contemporaries in Ravenna, which represents the Transfiguration of Jesus Christ.

Access to the library is restricted, owing to the past disappearance of rare manuscripts in Arabic, Syrian, Latin and Coptic. Outside the walls is the Charnel House, which displays the bones of departed monks.

Within the fortress walls is a mosque built in the early 12th century. The monastery has been respected by all the armies which later crossed Sinai — including a guarantee of immunity from the forces of Islam, and the fact that General Kléber of Napoleon's army helped repair the fortress walls.

Dedication to St. Catherine came many years after the establishment of the monastery. St. Catherine was born in Alexandria in 294 AD and was named Dorothea by her pagan family. Her wealthy father paid a monk to give her private tuition in the sciences, philosophy, medicine and poetry. When the holy man recognised the high intelligence of his pupil, he also instructed her in the tenets of Christianity. Dorothea was converted, and took the Christian name of Catherine.

This infuriated her father, who tried to persuade her to return to her original pagan upbringing. But father did not succeed. Attacking the Emperor for idolatry, Catherine was tortured on a spiked wheel (better remembered today as a Catherine wheel) and was finally beheaded. According to legend, angels transported her dead body to the highest point of the Sinai peninsula — the location which is now called St. Catherine's Mountain, and is higher than Mount Sinai by 200 metres.

Centuries later the monks found her body on the mountain, installed the relics in their basilica, and renamed the monastery.

Mount Sinai

For the energetic, a variation on the Monastery excursion is to leave overnight for St. Catherine's, and to climb the 2285-metre peak of Mount Sinai by torchlight, in time for a dramatic sunrise. You can go up by camel-track and down by the 3,750 granite Steps of Repentance. It has been suggested that an Eleventh Commandant should be added: "Take away thy litter from the mountain," which is sacred to Jews, Christians and Muslims alike.

Exploring the desert

Visitors to Sharm el Sheikh will be struck by the sharp contrast between the rich marine life on the coral reefs and the seemingly barren desert. But — besides the 'obligatory' trip to St. Catherine's Monastery — it's worth sampling some of the desert excursions arranged by local agencies, to get a closer view of the austere beauty of the Sinai Peninsula. There are Bedouin Dinners on offer, or whole-day excursions to the Coloured Canyon or to the Mangrove Forest of Nabeq.

7.4 Al Quseir

As the nearest Red Sea port to Luxor, Al Quseir has an extremely long history. At Luxor, one of the highlights is a visit to the Queen Hatshepsut Temple, where bas-reliefs dating from the 15th century BC depict a major trading expedition which set forth in a fleet of galleys from the present-day port, down the east coast of Africa to what probably was Somalia.

For 3500 years, the port continued to handle import-export business between the Upper Nile Valley and the Red Sea, and pilgrim traffic en route to Mecca. In more modern times, most of that transport business has been captured by the Suez Canal, though the port still handles local export of phosphates.

Today the old camel trail through the Eastern desert and mountains between Luxor, Qift and Al Quseir is followed by a modern highway for the 5-hour journey. The line of the ancient route was firmly settled during the reign of Ramses IV (1164-1157 BC), with a series of wells dug to serve the caravans.

When the Ottoman Empire absorbed Egypt in 1517, a small fort was built during the reign of Selim the Grim, to overlook the town.

Thanks to its excellent beach and opportunities for snorkelling and scuba-diving, El Quadim Bay — about 3 miles north of Al Quseir town — now brings new life and prospects to the 4,000 inhabitants of Al Quseir.

The very peaceful and relaxed beachside resort provides a different view of Egypt from sightseeing of the historic Nile. A Friday market brings in Bedouins from the desert.

Hurghada

Further north up the Red Sea coast is Hurghada, where the coastal fringes are emerald green with small islands and coral reefs. From the purist view of the more dedicated fish- and coral-watching divers, the reefs have been damaged or are severely stressed. But they are still superb for the average goggler by snorkel or glass-bottom boat.

Now being built are several new top-grade hotels which will certainly improve the attraction of the resort when building is completed. Meanwhile the resort is best left to the sub-aqua and watersport enthusiasts, for whom there is a full range of relatively low-cost diving and sport facilities. The most popular coral-viewing excursions are to the reefs around Geftun Island.

For beginners: an open water PADI certified diving course lasting between 4 and 5 days and including 9 dives and all equipment is priced at about £200 sterling.

7.5 Watersport and coral

The main rule for divers and snorkellers is "look but don't touch". Corals are living animals that produce a skeleton. Under the right conditions — clear, warm (20 or more degrees C) water — these animals thrive and produce coral reefs. Reefs in the Ras Mohammed National Park contain up to 150 different species of coral animals.

These provide the basis for an eco-system that supports large numbers of associated animals and plants, all living in fine balance. The coral reef is a complex and fragile system in which all its constituent parts are interconnected and interdependent.

The coral has within it a single-celled algae. This algae or plant, like all plants, converts sunlight to energy which is used for growth and reproduction. Without the coral, all other animals would be reduced to very low numbers.

Hard corals grow continuously given the right conditions, faster in summer than in winter. As they grow, they are also being eroded from within by sponges, bivalves and other animals. Growth will exceed erosion in a healthy coral reef. But corals grow slowly: 3 to 7.5 cms per year under optimum conditions. Soft corals, though beautiful, do not contribute energy to the coral reef system. They are often found in large numbers on damaged coral reef areas.

Since coral reefs attract and retain large numbers of fish, they also attract large numbers of divers intent on enjoying this beautiful environment. But uncontrolled use always leads to damage, and eventually the death of the coral reef. Hence there are strict rules for visitors and dive boat operators. Anchoring on reef areas, all kinds of fishing and removal of coral are prohibited.

Don't feed the fish

Park rangers closely watch diving and snorkelling activity. Fish feeding — to encourage fish to rise to the surface for the pleasure of snorkellers — is banned. It's even taboo to wash dishes aboard, as that becomes another way of fish feeding. Human food is not the normal diet of fish, which can quickly become dependent and aggressive.

National Park management ensures that beach hotels make nil pollution, with strict control of sewage and garbage disposal. Because of all this close supervision, the water quality is excellent.

Even non-divers can enjoy the magic of the coral reef aboard a glass-bottomed boat. Every detail is visible in the crystal-clear water, a hundred feet down to the sandy bottom. Gorgeous fish of every colour, shape and size dart and twist in an underwater three-dimensional ballet. The boats do not seem to disturb their normal life. Many fish approach within inches of the glass, almost nuzzling it. There is similar fabulous beauty about the coral itself, a living reef resplendent with colour and sinuous movement.

To recognise all the dazzling display of underwater life, a fish-watcher's field guide on a single sheet of plastic costs about one pound sterling in hotel shops. Most of the listed fish would be seen by an experienced diver on virtually any of the coral reefs, within an 80-metre range of a diving location.

Finally, a reminder: luggage is X-rayed on departure from Sharm el Sheikh airport, and any corals removed. As a result, some people have then missed flights and had to pay fines.

Chapter Eight
Further reference

8.1 History and Myth

Dates across the centuries
All the dates and dynasties, deities and pharaohs become very confusing to the layman — especially when all the details are poured forth by guides who have absorbed the background through a lifetime. In 3rd century BC, an Egyptian historian called Manetho divided the sequence of ruling families of ancient Egypt into thirty royal dynasties from Menes to Alexander the Great. These dynasties were later grouped into three main periods:

(1) The Old Kingdom, when the pyramids were built;
(2) The Middle Kingdom;
(3) The New Kingdom.

Modern historians have subdivided these three 'kingdoms' still further, and extended the periods from the Romans to the present day. Here's a basic outline.

Pre-Dynastic period: up to 3100 BC
Palaeolithic and Neolithic remains show that the Nile valley was inhabited for thousands of prehistoric years. In those times, rainfall was plentiful, and the Nile wider. Tribes settled in the Delta and Middle Egypt, growing wheat, barley and flax, herding sheep and goats, and weaving cloth. Successors learned the skills of farming, pottery, mining and the working of gold, silver and copper. Later, irrigation schemes were developed. They used a 365-day calendar, but left no written records.

The Old Kingdom: 1st to 6th Dynasties, 3100-2181 BC. Menes, or Mena, was the first king of the 1st Dynasty. He united Upper and Lower Egypt, and made Memphis the capital. The original Step Pyramid at neighbouring Sakkara was built during King Zoser's reign in the Third Dynasty; other pyramids and the Sphinx during the Fourth Dynasty. Temples to Ra, the Sun God, were built from the 5th

Dynasty, and religion was linked with kingship. Rulers from the 6th Dynasty onwards were called 'son of Ra', to cement their claim to be part human, part divine.

First Intermediate Period: 7th to early 11th Dynasties, 2181-2050 BC. A turbulent Dark Age, when a mere 130 years saw the coming and going of four Dynasties.

The Middle Kingdom: late 11th, and 12th Dynasties, 2050-1786 BC: Unity of Upper and Lower Egypt was restored, and Egyptian civilization flowered during this age of prosperity. Nubia, Lebanon and Libya were colonized. The capital was moved to Thebes.

Second Intermediate Period: 13th to 17th Dynasties, 1786-1567 BC. Another historic low point, when the Hyskos tribes invaded from Asia, using the new technology of horse-drawn war chariots. They subjugated northern Egypt, while Theban kings of the 17th Dynasty held on to the south.

New Kingdom: 18th to 20th Dynasties, 1567-1085 BC. The Asian invaders were driven out by a powerful and reorganized army which went on to conquer new territories. This period is richly documented, thanks to tomb and temple paintings and inscriptions.

The greatest pharaohs from this period were Queen Hatshepsut, Thutmost III, Akhenaten (husband of Nefertiti), Seti I and Ramses II. Temples were decorated with triumphant scenes of battle led by warriors Seti and his son Ramses. The boy-king Tutankhamun, who ruled 1361 to 1352 BC, died too young (age 19) to make his mark on history. But he was buried in a tomb that defied grave-robbers until the world-famed treasures were discovered in 1922, and relocated in the Egyptian Museum in Cairo.

Decadence Period: 21st to 24th Dynasties, 1085-750 BC. Yet another 'dark age' of weak rulers and foreign invasions. The empire shrank, royal building projects were abandoned, and corruption flourished during a period of sporadic civil wars.

The Late Egyptian Period: 25th to 30th Dynasties, 751-332 BC. Nubian kings took over part of Upper Egypt. Assyrian invaders were finally expelled by the Egyptians helped by Greek mercenaries. But then Egypt came under Persian rule from 525 to 404 BC, and again from 341 to 333 BC. During that period Babylon-in-Egypt was built — today's 'Old Cairo'.

The Ptolemies: 332 BC to 30 BC

Alexander the Great arrived with his triumphant Greek army in 332 BC, ended the Persian occupation, and stayed just long enough to adopt the local religion and the title of pharaoh. When Alexander died in 323 BC, his generals carved up the empire.

Ptolemy (Ptolemy I) took over Egypt, and established a Macedonian dynasty with Greek as the official language, but with adherence to Egyptian religion. The Ptolemies came increasingly under Roman control in 1st century BC. The last of the Ptolemies was Cleopatra VII (51-30 BC), whose story has been popularised by Shakespeare, Bernard Shaw and Hollywood.

Roman Period: 30 BC to 395 AD

Following the naval defeat of Anthony and Cleopatra at Actium, Egypt became a province of the Roman empire. Garrisons were established at Alexandria, Old Cairo and Aswan, mainly to guard trade routes and ensure delivery of grain to Rome. Otherwise, traditional Egyptian life continued, with Alexandria as an on-going centre of Greek culture.

Temples were built, in a hybrid of Egyptian, Greek and Roman styles. The cult of Isis flourished in Rome, while St. Mark introduced the subversive religion of Christianity to first-century Egypt. Coptic Christians clashed with Roman rulers who responded with persecution, particularly during the reign of Diocletian (284-305).

Christianity was legalised in 313, and became the official state religion of the Roman empire. But the Coptic church was regarded as heretical, and went its own way. Desert monasteries were established.

Byzantine Period: 395-641

The Roman empire split, and Egypt became part of the Byzantine empire, which weakly ruled from Constantinople — present-day Istanbul. The Coptic church flourished, and worship of the ancient gods faded away.

Arab Dynasties: 641-1517

Arab invaders defeated a Byzantine army at Memphis, and soon established modern-day Cairo as their capital. The Islamic faith spread rapidly, though Coptic Christians were tolerated. A succession of Arab dynasties followed, mostly of relatively short duration. The warrior Salah al Din (aka Saladin) grasped power in 1171, founded his own Ayyubids Dynasty, defeated the Crusaders and built Cairo's Citadel. The Mameluke Dynasties lasted longest, from 1250-1517.

Ottoman Period: 1517-1798

The Mamelukes were conquered by the Turks under Selim the Grim, and Egypt became a province of the Ottoman empire. But there was little change in Egyptian affairs and life-style. The Mameluke aristocracy continued as virtual rulers, at the cost of a steady flow of tax revenues to Constantinople. Otherwise there was stagnation and decay in the public sector.

French Period: 1798-1802

Napoleon landed with 25,000 troops and 150 scholars, scientists and artists. Alexandria and Cairo were rapidly captured, followed by Upper Egypt a few months later. Nelson's navy then bottled the French into Egypt, while Napoleon's scholars laid the basis of modern Egyptology.

A key discovery by French military engineers was the Rosetta Stone. This contained a decree issued in 196 BC and written both in Egyptian and Greek. The Egyptian version was written twice, in hieroglyphics and in demotic — a cursive development of the hieroglyphic script.

French scholars guessed that the contents of the three texts were identical. Only the Greek, however, could be understood, as all knowledge of hieroglyphic writing had been lost since the 4th century AD, and of demotic shortly afterward. The Rosetta Stone led directly to decyphering of the hieroglyphs, opening up the entire written history of ancient Egypt. When the French troops surrendered to the British, handing over the Rosetta Stone was written into the terms. The prize is now a treasured exhibit in the British Museum.

8.2 Who's who among the gods

For the non-Egyptologist, all the sacred animals, gods and goddesses become extremely confusing. The guides know them all intimately by name, but it's hard to remember who is who. All gods and goddesses have a symbol — usually of an animal or bird. Here's a brief check-list.

Amun: Lord of the Gods — the 'hidden one', and the father of the kings. The cult god of Thebes, worshipped at the Karnak Temple, which is his official residence. In Luxor Temple he has an annual 17-day honeymoon with his wife, Mut.

Amun-Ra: King of the gods, a blending of sun-god Ra with Amun.

Anubis: The son of Nephthys, he is the jackal-headed god of the necropolis — the god of mummification — black in colour.

Anukis: A bird looking like an egret, considered to bring the sun every morning, and would stand on the top of the obelisk.

Aten: The unique god briefly established by king Akhenaten and Queen Nefertiti. He was portrayed as a sun disc, with rays that ended with hands that offered life and prosperity to the people.

Atum: The god of eternity — one of the head gods during the Old Kingdom, and was creator of the rest of the gods of that time.

Bastet: A Late Period mother goddess, symbolised as a cat, the goddess for fun and music.

Edjo: A god of the earth during the Old Kingdom.

Eos: A local god worshipped in Bani Hassan, in the form of a dog.

Geb: God of earth, son of Shu (god of air) and brother of Nut (sky goddess).

Haroeris: Worshipped in Greek and Roman times in Kom Ombo. In falcon shape, and represented the sun.

Hathor: Cow goddess of beauty, joy, love, dance and music. She is portrayed either as a woman with cow's ears or horns, and a solar disc. She also symbolises fertility.

Horus: The falcon-headed son of Isis and Osiris. Originally he was god of the sky, and his eyes were the sun and the moon. He avenged the murder of his father, and regained supreme power over the earth from his wicked uncle Seth. The pharaohs claimed their right to rule on the basis that they were the incarnation of Horus.

Ihy: The god of the necropolis, one of the four gods in the shape of a dog.

Isis: Goddess of maternity, and love, the wife of Osiris. Also the goddess of magic, coming in different shapes. The mother of Horus.

Khumn: Creative god who creates human beings on his potters wheel. In ram's head form.

Khonsu: Son of Mut and Amun, Khonsu travelled the night sky as god of the moon, and was often depicted with a hawk's head. As a prophet, he assisted Thoth the god of wisdom.

Maat: Goddess of truth and justice, who kept the universe in harmony. Recognised by the feather on her head.

Min: God of fertility; always shown with two feathers, and an erect male member.

Montu: God of war, in human shape.

Mut: The vulture-head wife of Amun, to whom she was married in the XVIII Dynasty. The goddess of nature, she lived at the Luxor Temple.

The next four ladies are protective goddesses. They created the sarcophagus of the kings with their protective wings.

Neith
Nekhbet
Selket
Nepthys: She helped her sister Isis to resurrect Osiris, and is the goddess of the funerary rites.
Nut: Goddess of the sky, with a body that stretched from horizon to horizon. Her father, Shu — god of air — held her up. Nut gave birth to the sun every morning, and swallowed the sun every night. She married Geb, god of the earth, and they had four children whose lives form the basis of ancient mythology — Seth, Isis, Osiris and Nepthys.
Opet: The goddess of feasting. Mostly came with Amun when he spent his annual honeymoon at Luxor Temple. Hence the occasion was called the Feast of Opet.

Osiris: God of vegetation, Osiris was married to his sister Isis. He was killed by his jealous brother, Seth, who cut his body into 14 parts and scattered them all over Egypt. Isis recovered the pieces, joined them together, and mummified the body. Thereafter Osiris was resurrected, and ruled the underworld.
Ptah: The God who created the world — was worshipped in Memphis, the first capital of ancient Egypt. He spoke the name of each thing, and thus created by word of mouth. But his wife, Sekhmet, was the war goddess.
Ra: The mighty sun-god, the supreme creator often fused with other gods.
Ra-Harakhty: A combination of Ra with the falcon-god Horus. He opened the gates for the kings to embark on the journey to their second life.
Satis: One of the local animals worshipped in Akhenaten's time.
Sekhmet: The lion-headed goddess of war, and wife of Ptah, the creator god.
Serapis: In the form of a bull, the god of power and strength.
Seshat: Goddess of writing — she always wrote nice things about the king. She had a star-shaped crown.
Seth: The murderer of Osiris, Seth was finally exiled into the wilderness. The evil one, god of mountains and deserts.
Shu: God of the air, who held up his daughter Nut, goddess of the sky.
Sobek: Crocodile god of the flood, and was greatly feared.
Thoth: An ibis-headed intellectual — god of writing and wisdom, who helped judge the dead. Her symbol was an ibis.
Wepwawet: 'The Opener', the god who opened the gates for the kings to go to the second life.

8.3 The Egypt of today

Changing course

By the early 19th century, most possessions of the Ottoman Empire had fallen into stagnation. Any western-style Industrial Revolution was a non-starter. In Egypt, 1805, power was grasped by Mohammed Ali, an Albanian soldier in the Ottoman army. He ruled as Pasha — as a viceroy theoretically under Ottoman control. In his moves to create a modern Egypt, he found his policies blocked by the power structure of the Mamelukes. Most of the aristocracy was invited to a feast by Mohammed Ali in 1811, and massacred on their way home — a farewell banquet for 470. Any remaining Mamelukes throughout Egypt met the same fate, but without the prior courtesy of a good meal.

Mohammed Ali then injected European know-how to modernise Egypt — building canals, railways, factories and a better-organised army. He introduced the new cash crop of cotton, and died insane in 1849.

Among his successors, Said Pasha gave the French a concession to build a Suez canal, completed in 1869. But high spending on modernisation of Cairo led close to national bankruptcy. The British government bought up the available Suez Canal shares in 1875.

British control and Nationalism: 1882-1952

Financial and other disorders continued, and Britain finally sent in the gunboats in 1882. Although Egypt theoretically remained part of the Ottoman Empire until World War I, in practice it was a British protectorate, and virtually a colony. Nationalism flourished, and finally in 1922 Britain recognised Egypt as an independent monarchy. Fouad, the khedive of Egypt, became king, but Britain still kept control of defence, law, communications and operation of the Suez Canal. In 1936 a new treaty with King Farouk gave full independence to Egypt, but with British forces remaining in the Suez Canal Zone.

During World War II, Egypt became Britain's prime military base for North Africa and Middle East, with the battle of el-Alamein as the key turning-point.

Modern Egypt

Egypt's 1948 defeat by Israel heightened discontent with incompetence and corruption at the top. In 1952 a bloodless coup by General Naguib — backed by a Revolutionary Command Council led by Colonel Nasser — deposed King Farouk. Nasser was proclaimed president in 1956, and headed a domestic and international policy of Arab socialism and Arab unity.

Pre-1952, Egypt's economy was based on farming, with relatively little industry. New policies were aimed at expanding the economy through State action. There was redistribution of feudal estates to landless peasants — the fellaheen. The most ambitious project was to build the Aswan High Dam. But a US veto of World Bank loans led directly to the 1956 Suez Crisis which left Nasser as a hero of the Arab world.

In 1961 the Government nationalized banking, insurance, mining, power production and transport. The economy was severely hit by the 1967 Six Day War with Israel. When Sadat became president after Nasser's death in 1970, many policies were reversed. Socialist laws were replaced by a new emphasis on private enterprise, and Soviet advisors were sent packing.

In turn, Egypt became more dependent on aid and investment from the West, especially following an Arab League aid boycott after the 1978 Camp David peace treaty with Israel. Muslim fundamentalists assassinated Sadat in 1981. Since then, President Mubarak has followed the basic line of Sadat's policies, especially to maintain close links with USA, the principal source of western aid. The pay-back came with Egyptian support in the Gulf War of 1990-91. Today, Egypt's budget relies heavily on revenues from sources that can be highly erratic, dependent on world conditions: petroleum exports, Suez Canal tolls, remittances from expatriates, and from tourism.

Women

Until the 1920's, the veil was worn in public by all respectable middle-class and upper-class women, whether they were Muslim, Jewish or Christian. It had no special religious meaning.

By the mid-30's, however, veils had become a comparative rarity in Egypt, though they continued as fashion items in Syria and Jordan for another thirty years. But they have remained compulsory in the Arabian peninsula to this day.

In modern-day Egypt, veils are worn mainly by Bedouin women or by the younger urban middle-class who wish to display either modesty or Muslim piety.

Egyptian women have now entered professions such as law, medicine and diplomacy, but they still do not have equality with men.

Etiquette

Egyptians are a very friendly and warm people. They will go out of their way to help you. But be patient. Things don't always go to plan. Egyptians also take their time when greeting each other before they get down to business.

Although alcohol is permitted in Egypt, do remember it is a Muslim country. Drink moderately. Laws relating to gambling are more flexible than in some other Muslim countries, but hotel casinos are primarily intended for the amusement of foreign visitors.

8.4 Looking at architecture

The survival of Egyptian architecture is due to its essential simplicity, and monumental use of huge masses of stone or granite, set with great precision. Domestic architecture, based on use of mud-brick, has left no trace. It has all returned back to the original Nile silt.

Before your exposure to a stream of architectural terms from the guides, here's a summary of the main technical words:

Bas-reliefs — a technique of carving back from the stone surface, to leave the sculpture projecting slightly from the background. In contrast are 'sunk' reliefs, carved into the stone. Many of the reliefs were brightly painted.

Chapels — side rooms for storage, or for worship of lesser deities.

Colonnades — a feature of open courts, with the individual columns often richly decorated, and designed in the form of palms, or the budding or flowering stalks of papyrus or lotus. Some early (3,000 BC) fluted columns resemble the much later Greek Doric.

Colossi — extremely large statues.

Cult temples — specialised in worship of the most-favoured god of the region.

Hypostyle hall — a hall with roofing slabs supported by a thick forest of columns.

Mastabas — A rectangular cut stone tomb with sloping walls and a flat roof, usually containing three chambers. The first was richly decorated with paintings; the second portrayed the deceased high-ranking personality; the third, where the mummy was laid.

Mortuary temple — dedicated to the memory of a dead pharaoh.

Obelisks — monolithic monuments to the sun god, glittering at the tip with gold or an alloy of gold and silver.

Pillars — supports that were normally square in section, often with sculptures on each face — especially of the pharaoh, portrayed as the god Osiris.

Precincts — the surrounding area of a temple, usually enclosed within high mud-brick walls, and occupied by priests, workrooms and general storage.

Pylon — monumental gateway at a temple entrance.

Rock-cut tombs and monuments — Temples and tombs cut into the natural rock: Abu Simbel is the best-known example.

Sacred Lake — located within the temple precincts, for ritual ablutions.

Sanctuary — the innermost shrine of a temple, housing the god's statue, to which only high priests and pharaohs were admitted for the making of offerings and sacrifice.

Step pyramid — the earliest form of pyramid, located at Sakkara, without the smooth limestone casing of subsequent pyramids.

Vestibule — an antechamber that marked the final approach to the temple sanctuary.

Quick guide to the temples

Abu Simbel — The most impressive of them all, glorifying its builder, Ramses II. Like Philae, it was saved from its original flooded site. (See p. 83).

Abydos — Dedicated to Osiris, built by Seti I, and completed by his son Ramses II. Very colourful, north of Luxor.

Deir el-Bahri — the mortuary temple of Queen Hatshepsut, on Luxor's West Bank. (See p. 62).

Dendarah — Dedicated to Hathor, the cow-headed goddess, the wife of Horus. (See p. 88).

Edfu — Dedicated to Horus, the falcon headed god, son of Isis and Osiris; the most complex temple of them all. (See p. 87).

Esna — Dedicated to Khnum, god of creation. Just a small but colourful hypostyle hall remains. (See p. 87).

Karnak — Dedicated to Ra, the sun god, and the most extensive of all sites. (See p. 57).

Kom Ombo — Dedicated to two gods — Horus and Sobek (the crocodile-headed god). Each god has his own sanctuary. (See p. 87).

Luxor — Only two miles from Karnak, and likewise dedicated to Ra. (See p. 55).

Philae — An island temple at Aswan, dedicated to Isis. (See p. 74).

Ramasseum — A stupendous mortuary temple to the eternal memory of Ramses II. (See p. 61).

8.5 The world of Islam

Mosques

Mosque design follows a set pattern. In the spacious courtyard are fountains for ritual ablutions before the faithful go in to pray. Carpets totally cover the floor. A niche called mihrab indicates the direction of Mecca. From an elaborate pulpit, the imam delivers the Friday sermon.

Many mosques are beautifully decorated with tiles, but the Koran forbids any representation of living creatures. Designs are usually of formal geometric patterns, with possibly stylised flowers. Walls are often adorned with verses from the Koran in Arabic calligraphy, which few European visitors can read, but which look very pretty.

From minarets, looking like slim pencils against the skyline, loudspeakers call Muslims to prayer five times a day — a pre-dawn wake-up call, then at sunrise, noon, afternoon, sunset and evening. The *Egyptian Gazette* will normally give you the exact times to expect the call.

Sunshine retreat

Mosques are little havens of tranquillity. On stone benches around their courtyards, elderly greybeards pass the time in sunshine or shade, according to season. The 20th century seems far removed.

The basis of the Islamic religion is "submission to the will of Allah". The prophet Mohammed received the spoken word of Allah — the Koran — while in Mecca some time between 610 and 632 AD. Around 94% of Egyptians are Muslims: they do not like to be called Mohammedans.

Muslim life is governed by rules, laws and customs which are based on the five Pillars of Faith:

Shadada — To accept that "There is no God but Allah, and Mohammed is His Prophet."

Salah — To pray five times daily, in Arabic, facing Mecca.

Zakat — To give alms to the needy: between 2.5% and 10% of personal income.

Saum — To fast during Ramadan, the 9th month of the Muslim lunar year, when the Koran was revealed to Mohammed. Between dawn and sunset, believers must abstain from food, drink and smoking; and abstain from sex throughout the month. The day starts with a substantial pre-dawn breakfast, and ends with a splendid meal after sunset.

The Hadj — To make pilgrimage to Mecca at least once in a lifetime, if health and finances permit. It's a major source of passenger traffic for EgyptAir.

8.6 Egyptian cuisine

In general, hotels serve food that will appeal to European tastes. But, for the determined gourmet, there's great interest in trying spicier Egyptian dishes such as 'Kofta' — charcoal-grilled meatballs — or Fuul Beans, the staple diet of the Egyptians. All hotels offer vegetarian meals on request.

If you want to explore Arab cuisine, see below for some items to seek out. The anglicized spellings can vary, depending on how conversions are made from the Arabic, and how well the menu-writer can cope with English language.

Major influences on Egyptian food during the past thousand years have come from the classic cuisines of Persia, Syria, Lebanon and especially Ottoman Turkey, besides Italy, France and even England. Truly native dishes are based upon the ancient tradition of stewing vegetables.

Egyptian Hors d'Oeuvres, salads or garnishes are known as **Mezze**. If you order a selection, at least a dozen little platters could arrive — often enough for a complete meal. Mezze are eaten with fingers, or scooped up in pieces of flat pita bread.

Here's a typical selection from an oriental or Lebanese restaurant: fuul mesdames (see below); goat cheese; vine leaves stuffed with rice; lentils with rice and fried onions; parsley, lemon, crushed wheat and tomato; egg-plant; yoghurt with crushed nuts; oriental salad with crispy bread; chickpeas; fave beans; stuffed peppers; fried humus and chicken wings.

Beans with everything

There are many variations on bean dishes, at least 57.

Fuul — the local beans, boiled and mashed with varied additions such as egg, meat, onion, oil or lemon. As a light snack, often eaten as a pita-bread sandwich.

Taameyya or **Falafel** — balls of minced white broad beans with onions, garlic and coriander, deep fried and served hot with tehina. There are many variations, some with eggs or minced meat.

Fuul medammes — baked beans seasoned with olive oil, lemon and crushed garlic.

Tehina — sesame seed paste mixed with water and lemon juice, eaten as a dip with pita bread.

Tehina salad — salted cucumber, lettuce and sliced tomatoes with olive oil, lemon juice and dressed in tehina.

Hummus — a creamy dip made from puréed chickpeas.

Baba ghannoug — roasted aubergine mashed with tehina and crushed garlic.
Dolma — white or black aubergines, stuffed with rice etc.
Mahshi — Arab equivalent of the Turkish or Greek dolma: aubergines, vine or cabbage leaves stuffed with rice, minced meat, onions etc.

Main courses are mostly meat dishes of which the following are the most popular:
Shwarma — sliced lamb, packed on a rotating skewer to be charcoal-grilled.
Kufta — charcoal-grilled meatballs of minced lamb or mutton mixed with chopped onions, parsley and spices.
Mulukhia — lamb or chicken cooked in a soup of the aromatic mulukhia plant, with garlic and coriander, and served with rice.
Hamam fil tagen — grilled pigeons stuffed with rice and cream.
Kebabs — mainly diced lamb or beef cooked on skewers. There is also a chicken version known as chicken Taouk.

Vegetarian dishes — apart from the choice of non-meat mezzes, salads, mashed or fried bean dishes and the usual run of omelettes, try some of these:
Fataya — baked spinach pastry.
Fattett Moulukhiya — cooked leafy green vegetable and rice.
Labna — thick, soft yoghurt like cheese.
Waraq Anab — vine leaves stuffed with rice and lentils.

Desserts are mostly extremely sweet, swimming in sugar syrup. If you don't have an excessively sweet tooth, stay with the excellent choice of fresh fruit.
Mahallabiyya — a rice or corn flour pudding, sometimes topped with cinnamon.
Oom Ali — pastry baked with milk, raisins and nuts, like a rich bread and butter pudding, greatly recommended.

Drinks

Because Egypt is predominately Muslim, alcohol is not widely available. EgyptAir is a teetotal airline, and many average-grade restaurants serve soft drinks only. However, the principal hotels, leading restaurants and cruise-boats can all offer a selection of alcoholic beverages. But don't expect any bargains in the wine lists.

Most wines and spirits have to be imported, so they are expensive. Regrettably, Egypt does not have any great wine-making tradition. Egyptian wines like Omar El Khayyam (dry red) and Cru des Ptolémées (dry white) are worth trying maybe once, though chronic wine-drinkers usually make do with the rosé Rubis d'Egypte. If you're desperate, try improving the taste with 7-Up or soda. Classic European wines have no fear of potential competition.

A better bet is the Egyptian-brewed beer. The leading brands are Stella Lager (also known as Stella local) and Stella Export, brewed and bottled by the Pyramids Beverage Company and served ice-cold. Stella local comes in a half-litre or 1-litre bottle, with lowish alcohol content. Stella Export is in a much smaller bottle, is stronger, and is double the price of Stella local.

Costing twice as much again is imported canned beer. If you just order "beer", the waiter will automatically bring you the most expensive German import in stock. Most visitors find that Stella local is the best buy for dehydration purposes, though some hotels claim they don't stock it.

Drinking the water

Especially during the hotter months, most visitors absorb large quantities of bottled water. Because of the dry atmosphere, doctors advise drinking 8 to 10 glasses of non-alcoholic liquid per day. The main beneficiary of this advice is the Baraka brand of natural water from a deep well, bottled in association with Vittel. A rival brand has links with Evian. On excursions, everyone soon gets the habit of always clutching a 1½-litre bottle as lifeline against the desert sun.

A standard 1.5 litre plastic bottle of water costs maybe LE 2.20 plus taxes in hotels; LE 2 in supermarkets; LE 1.50 from street vendors if you haggle them down from a starting price of LE 2 or 3.

Among Egyptians themselves, mint tea and coffee are the most popular drinks. The coffee arrives thick and black in Turkish style, and served *saada* (without sugar), medium or sweet. If you don't specify, it will be sweet. Tea, likewise. Nescafé is always available.

Otherwise, juice bars offer excellent choice of thirst-quenchers. According to season, try freshly squeezed and chilled strawberry, mango, lemon, guava, grapefruit, banana, pomegranate, lime, orange, carrot or sugar-cane. Or, for a mixture of flavours, order a fruit-juice cocktail.

Less recommended is a sweet red drink called Karkadeh, made from dried hibiscus flower. It could be ideal as a mouthwash, but some people like it. Coke, Pepsi and 7-Up are everywhere.

Finally, to minimise stomach upsets, re-read the hints in the 'Medical' section in chapter one.

8.7 Learn some Arabic

Arabic is the official language of Egypt, and is the mother tongue of over eighty million people throughout North Africa and the Middle East. The language originated in the Arabian Peninsula and spread north and west with the rise of Islam.

Spoken Arabic today is classified into six major groups:

The classic language: Has undergone only minor changes in the Arabian Peninsula itself. Classic Arabic is the speech of all inhabitants of that region, both nomads and town dwellers.

The Mediterranean Dialect: Closest to the classic language, is spoken throughout Jordan, Israel, Lebanon and Syria.

The Iraqi Dialect: Is marked by the use of additional words and expressions from Kurdish, Persian and Turkish.

The Cairo Dialect: Spoken in most parts of Lower Egypt.

The Southern Nile Valley Dialect: Arabic of the Sudan and Upper Egypt, closer to the classic language.

The North African Dialect: spoken in Libya, Tunisia, Morocco and Algeria — the four lands of the Maghreb (which means the West).

Try out some Arabic

Most Egyptians in hotel or tourism business speak English or French. But it always adds pleasure if you can attempt an occasional word or phrase — even if it sounds like a remote dialect!

Please — Min Fadlak
Thank you — Shukran
Never mind — Mahlesh
Good Morning — Sabah el Kheir
Good Evening — Mesai el Kheir
How do you do — Ahlahn wah sahlahn
How are you — Izzayak
Goodbye — Maa el Salama
Good night — Tesbah el khay
Today — Eneharda
Tomorrow — Bukra
I — Anah
You — Entah
Yes — Iwah
No — La'a
How much — Becam
Money — Faloos

No change	— Mafeesh fak-kah
What time is it	— Issa a kam
Taxi	— Sayyaarat
Luggage	— Am-teea
Passport	— Jawaaz-safar
Salt	— Melah
Pepper	— Fil-fil
Water	— Em-maya
Tea	— Shay
Coffee	— Awah
Milk	— Leban
Knife	— Moos or sekeen
Fork	— Shauka
Hot	— Hahr
Cold	— Bard
Toilet	— Wc or twalet
Chemist	— Sai daliya
Bank	— Mas-raf
Post Office	— Al-bareed
Stamps	— Taba-bareed
Telephone	— Haatif
The bill please	— Al-hisaab min-fadlak
Don't mention it	— Af-wan

8.8 Further reading

For anyone who wants a deeper understanding of ancient Egypt, every public library offers a wide range of books on Egyptology. In Egypt itself there are numerous books with excellent colour reproductions. They enable you to study and recapture many of the finer details of temples and paintings. Other books can give you an insight into modern Egyptian life.

Among the factual publications, consider the following: "Khul-Khaal" — the stories of five different Egyptian women. "Shahhat, the Egyptian" — by Richard Critchfield: gives insight into peasant life in Upper Egypt today.

In the realm of fiction, you cannot do better than read the works of Naguib Mahfouz, who won the Nobel prize for literature in 1988. Many of his works have been translated into English. His best-known work is a trilogy: "Palace Walk", "Palace of Desire" and "Sugar Street".

There are many others, including "Adrift on the Nile" and a collection of short stories "The Time and the Place". Naguib Mahfouz has written over thirty novels and around a hundred short stories. Among Egyptians, possibly his most popular work is "Midaq Alley"

Any of these will make enjoyable reading and give you deeper understanding of modern Egypt and life in Cairo.

8.9 Learn Arabic numerals

Numbers

0	٠	sifr	10	١٠	'ashara
1	١	wahid	11	١١	hidashar
2	٢	itnein	12	١٢	itnashar
3	٣	talata	13	١٣	talatashar
4	٤	arb'a	14	١٤	arb'atashar
5	٥	khamsa	15	١٥	khamastashar
6	٦	sitta	16	١٦	sittashar
7	٧	sab'a	17	١٧	saba'tashar
8	٨	tamanya	18	١٨	tamantashar
9	٩	tis'a	19	١٩	tisa'tashar

20	٢٠	'ashreen	100	١٠٠	miyya
21	٢١	wahid wi'ashreen	101	١٠١	miyya wi wahid
22	٢٢	itnein wi'ashreen	150	١٥٠	miyya we-khamseen
30	٣٠	talatin	200	٢٠٠	mitayn
40	٤٠	arba'in	500	٥٠٠	khamsa miyya
50	٥٠	khamseen	1000	١٠٠٠	alf
60	٦٠	sitteen	2000	٢٠٠٠	alfein
70	٧٠	sab'aeen	3000	٣٠٠٠	talat alaaf
80	٨٠	tamaneen	4000	٤٠٠٠	arba alaaf
90	٩٠	tis'een	5000	٥٠٠٠	khamsa alaaf